# Primer of Sidereal Astrology

Cyril Fagan
and
Brigadier R. C. Firebrace

Copyright 1971 by Roy Firebrace and Pauline Fagan

All rights reserved.

No part of this book may be reproduced or transmitted in any form or any means, electronic or mechanical, including photocopying or recording, or by any information storage and retrieval system, without written permission from the author and publisher. Requests and inquiries may be mailed to the American Federation of Astrologers, Inc., 6535 S. Rural Road, Tempe AZ 85283.

First Printing: London
First US Printing: 1971
Sixth US Printing: 2008

ISBN-10: 0-86690-427-1
ISBN-13: 978-0-86690-427-8

Cover Design: Jack Cipolla

Published by:
American Federation of Astrologers, Inc.
6535 S. Rural Road
Tempe AZ 85283

www.astrologers.com

Printed in the United States of America

It was my husband's hope that this book could be rewritten
and made more comprehensive.
But, alas, time ran out for Cyril Fagan before
this task had been accomplished.
However, this book in its present form with two new chapters added
fills a need for those who seek to study the subject seriously.

*Pauline Fagan*
*(Mrs. Cyril Fagan)*

# Contents

| | |
|---|---|
| Preface to Third Edition | vii |
| Preface to the First US Edition | ix |
| Abbreviations | x |
| Chapter I, Our City Universe | 1 |
| Chapter II, The Sidereal Zodiac | 7 |
| Chapter III, Conversion of a Tropical Map into the Sidereal | 15 |
| Chapter IV, The Mean Sun (M.S.) | 17 |
| Chapter V, The Calendar | 19 |
| Chapter VI, The Example Horoscope | 21 |
| Chapter VII, The Progressed Horoscope | 23 |
| Chapter VIII, Primary Directing of the Angles | 31 |
| Chapter IX, The Sidereal Solar Return (S.S.R.) | 35 |
| Chapter X, The Solar Quotidian Progression | 39 |
| Chapter XI, Progression of Solar Planets | 43 |
| Chapter XII, The Progressed Sidereal Solar Return (P.S.S.R.) | 49 |
| Chapter XIII, Regressions | 57 |
| Chapter XIV The Sidereal Lunar Return | 63 |
| Chapter XV The Anlunar Return | 67 |
| Chapter XVI Kinetic Returns | 69 |
| Chapter XVII Mundane Astrology | 77 |
| Chapter XVII, The Art of Interpretation | 81 |
| Appendix | 129 |
|     Calculation of Planets In Mundo | 129 |
|     Calculating Lunar Configurations | 132 |
|     Paranatellonta | 133 |
|     Precessing | 134 |
|     Notes on Tables | 135 |
|     Tables | 139 |

# Preface to the Third Edition

We have greatly extended the chapter on the vital subject of interpretation. We have retained in the Appendix methods of calculation and tables for the use of the keen student.

Methods of calculation employed with the sidereal zodiac have proved their worth and opened up the trail to a more accurate astrology freed from some medieval concepts. The student can easily convince himself or herself of this fact by a personal test. The student will find that the study of the ancient zodiac when taken with the new methods as well as with the older approved techniques will be both exciting and rewarding. We are convinced that an impartial study without fear, favour or affection will confirm our claims. They are put forward in this primer so that they can be tested by other astrologers and confirmed or rejected.

Our debt to Mrs. Joanne Clancy, the able editor of *American Astrology*, remains as she continues to publish in her magazine articles of great interest to the sidereal student. We are grateful to James Hynes of Dublin for permission to publish some of his excellent tables. To Garth Allen we are indebted for his work for sidereal astrology and in particular for his exact determination of the *ayanamsa*, a vital fact for sidereal astrology. Alexander Marr continues his research work into the sidereal and is responsible for the theory of regressions as applied to sidereal techniques. We are grateful too for his permission to publish in this book special tables designed to simplify the work of the student. Our debt to Mary Austin, our production manager, grows with each edition. Without her firm but gentle persuasion it is doubtful whether this book would have seen the light. Her Aquarian Sun knows how to compete with our respective Taurean and Leonian Suns. To her we owe the drawing of the maps which we use to illustrate our text.

We realize there is much still to learn about sidereal astrology, in particular in the field of interpretation. Time for research is always limited for any individual and we rely on students for the testing of our methods in order that we may learn a little more of our beloved astrology.

*Cyril Fagan*
*Roy Firebrace*
*London*

# Preface to the First US Edition

I welcome the publication of this new edition of *The Primer of Sidereal Astrology* by Cyril Fagan and myself. It has been out of print for some time. It now contains new matter from Cyril Fagan's pen. I feel this edition is In Memoriam to my friend and teacher, Cyril Fagan, who to the great loss to sidereal astrology is no longer with us.

This book will initiate its readers into the new delights of sidereal astrology which Cyril rediscovered for the world and taught to me. I am now more convinced than ever from my own research work that the sidereal zodiac is the true zodiac, and that through its use we can improve our astrology.

*Brigadier R.C. Firebrace*

## Abbreviations

| | |
|---|---|
| S.Z. | Sidereal Zodiac |
| T.Z. | Tropical Zodiac |
| S.V.P. | Synetic Vernal Point |
| S.S.R. | Sidereal Solar Return |
| S.S.I. | Sidereal Solar Ingress |
| S.L.R. | Sidereal Lunar Return |
| S.L.I. | Sidereal Lunar Ingress |
| S.N.Q. | Sidereal Natal Quotidian |
| S.N.Q.R. | Sidereal Natal Quotidian Regressed |
| S.Q. | Solar Quotidian |
| S.Q.R. | Solar Quotidian Regressed |
| P.S.S.R. | Progressed Sidereal Solar Return |
| R.S.S.R. | Regressed Sidereal Solar Return |
| S.K. | Solar Kinetic |
| N.Q.K. | Natal Quotidian Kinetic |
| N.Q.K.R. | Natal Quotidian Kinetic Regressed |
| S.T. | Sidereal time or Equinoctial Time |
| M.S. | Right Ascension of the Mean Sun (R.A.M.S.) |
| U.T. | Universal Time |
| A.T. | Astronomical Time |

# Chapter 1

# Our City-Universe

Among students of astrology it is common knowledge that the planets, asteroids and comets that compose our Solar System revolve around the Sun, each in its respective orbit, lying more or less in the plane of the ecliptic. This forms, as it were, a mighty disc, and is not unlike the appearance of a gramophone record, except that it is more elliptical than circular in shape. The planet furthermost from the Sun is Pluto, going slowly around the rim, while the innermost planet, Mercury, goes rapidly around the centre occupied by the Sun. The mean distance of the orbit of the Earth from the Sun is about 92,800,000 miles, and this distance is known as an "astronomical unit," such units being applicable to measurements made only within the Solar System. Thus, the mean distance of Mercury's orbit from the Sun is 0.39 astronomical units; Jupiter, 5.2; Saturn, 9.5; and Pluto, 39.5. In connection with measurements of vaster distances, astronomers use the light-year as the yardstick. Light travels at the rate of 186,324 miles a second; therefore, a "light-minute" is equivalent to 11 million miles. The Sun being about 93 million miles distant from the Earth, the light from it takes more than eight minutes to reach us. Consequently, we always see the Sun as it was some eight minutes ago. The same is true with Jupiter 40 minutes earlier; Saturn as it was over an hour ago; and Pluto five hours ago.

One light-year is equivalent to about six million million miles (5,878,500,500,000 miles). The distances of some of the familiar bright stars estimated in light-years from the Earth are shown at the right.

We see from this that Rigel, in "The Foot of Orion," is 500 light-years away from us, but, because it has 15,000 times the luminosity of our Sun, it appears in the night skies as a star of the first magnitude (m = minus 0.34). The brightest star in the heavens is, of

**Star Distance from Earth**

| Star | Light-years |
|---|---|
| Sirius | 8.6 |
| Altair | 16 |
| Pollux | 32 |
| Capella | 52 |
| Regulus | 56 |
| Aldebaran | 57 |
| Betelgeuse | 200 |
| Spica | 230 |
| Antares | 380 |
| Rigel | 500 |

course, Sirius—the Egyptian Sothis or Sepdet—with a magnitude of 1.58. This is not only because of its proximity to us (3.6 light-years) but also on account of its luminosity which is 26.3 times greater than that of our Sun. In our conceit, we are apt to think that the Sun is the biggest and brightest "thing" in creation, but this is very far from being so. In the vast assembly of fixed stars it is only a very modest, if not puny, unit; Betelgeuse and Omicron Ceti being 25 and 30 million times bigger, respectively.

When compared with the relatively rapid motions of the planets, or "wanderers" (as they are more literally termed), the fixed stars only *appear* to be fixed. In actual fact all the fixed stars have their own proper motions and they travel at gigantic speeds in different directions in space. But being so immensely far away, they appear on the average to move only one degree in about 120,000 years as viewed from Earth. The nearer the fixed stars are to the Solar System, the faster they appear to move. Thus Bungula, which enjoys about the same luminosity as our Sun, is only 4.3 light-years away, and consequently it moves one degree in about 1,900 years.

The multitude of fixed stars composing the various figures of the zodiacal and other constellations, plus the thousands (which includes our Sun with its brood of planets) visible to the naked eye, and the other teeming millions—to us only telescopic objects or obscured to view by cosmic dust—all are citizens of an immense City-Universe, each revolving at a different velocity and in unique orbit around its centre, forming a stupendous cosmic whirlpool. Known as the Galaxy, this "Island-Universe" contains about one hundred thousand million fixed stars, every one of which is a sun in its own right, the vast majority being embedded in its plane. Bounded about the rim by myriads of "suns" comprising the well-known Milky Way, our City-Universe is spiral and disc-like is shape, having many crescent-formed lanes of stars radiating from the centre, one of which contains most of the bright stars we see about us, Sun and planetary family included. This is about two-thirds of the distance from the hub, or about 30,000 light-years. With the exception of binaries, i.e., twin stars, gyrating very closely around each other, no fixed star revolves around another, but each and all, including the binaries, in their respective orbits, revolve around the centre of the Galaxy. Because of the presence of vast, dense clouds of cosmic dust, the centre of our Galaxy cannot be seen. But astronomers are of the opinion that City-Universes do not contain a central sun and that, in this respect, they differ from our Solar System. Sir James Jeans is of the opinion that the centres are filled with a dense crowd of ordinary stars holding one another together by their own gravitational pulls, and not controlled by a single central mass. In terms of the ancient Egypto-Babylonian zodiac, the centre of our City-Universe, detected by radioastronomy, lies at 2 Sagittarius 05 at latitude 5S32, and the pole of the Galaxy is in 6 Virgo 38 at latitude 29N49. The diameter of our City-Universe is estimated to be 75,000 light-years, i.e., light would take about 75,000 years to travel from rim to rim.

Eddington, in his *Expanding Universe,* estimates about one hundred thousand million City-Universes in existence, each containing a like number of fixed stars. The most powerful telescopes make galaxies appear as spiral nebulae. One of the nearest to us, and visible to the naked eye, is Vertex, the great nebular in the constellation Andromeda at 3 Aries 36 at latitude 33N21. It has a diameter of 130 light-years and is 2 million light-years distant from us. Its structure is not unlike our own City-Universe. The most distant known City-Universe lies in the constellation Bootes and it is estimated to be 4,500 million light-years away—a proof of the enormous antiquity and age of the Universe itself.

Together with its planetary escort, the Sun is swirling at the rate of 375 million miles a year and at a radius of some 30,000 light-years from the centre of our City-Universe. It is estimated some 220,000,000 years will pass before the completion of the circuit. The direction in the Galaxy taken by the sun is known as the "Solar Apex." The astrological world is greatly indebted to Garth Allen for bringing to its notice the latest determination of the position of this point in space made by two professors, A.N. Vyssotsky and Peter van de Kamp (vide *American Astrology*, August 1960). With regard to epoch 1950.0, they located it at right ascension 19h 00m and declination 36N00, plus or minus a maximum error of six minutes. If we reduce these tropical coordinates to those of the sidereal zodiac, it will be found that the minimum longitude is 26 Sagittarius 38, and mean 29 Sagittarius 24; maximum is 2 Capricorn 35 and mean latitude is 58N14. In short, the sidereal longitude of the mean position of the Apex lies a little over half a degree from 0 Capricorn of the ancient Egypto-Babylonian zodiac! There seems little doubt that when astronomers eventually succeed in determining the position of the Apex with greater precision, their result will be found to tally closely, if not precisely, with the longitude of 0 Capricorn as computed from Garth Allen's work, *S.V.P. Ephemeris.*

Astrologically speaking, this is one of the most important determinations of modern times. Why? Because it indubitably suggests that the zodiac of ancient Egypt, Bablyonia, Assyria, Chaldea and India had its fiducial in only one fixed star, namely, *the sun itself*, and not in any of its neighbours in the Galaxy. This seems all the more certain when it is remembered that no fixed star of any magnitude marked the commencement of any one of the four "cardinal" constellations. Relying on their *siddhantas,* Hindu astrologers maintained that Chita (Spica) heralded the beginning of Libra, and was therefore the fiducial star. But as the lists of the *yogataras* (or fixed stars) are, in the *siddhantas,* demonstrated as being tropical *(vide* "the Paranatellonta of Aswini," *The Astrological Magazine*, Bangalore, India, January and February 1952), no value can be set on their longitudes, especially so when Spica's longitude is given as 29 Virgo in the far more ancient Egyptian and Babylonian texts.

If we further reduce the tropical coordinates from the mean position of the apex for the epoch 1950.0 to epochs separated by intervals of 1,000 years, the following table is obtained:

| Epoch | R.A. | Declination |
|---|---|---|
| -4000 | 15h 35m | 42N14 |
| -3000 | 16h 08m | 39N13 |
| -2000 | 16h 40m | 36N55 |
| -1000 | 17h 16m | 35N27 |
| 0 | 17h 52m | 34N48 |
| +1000 | 18h 26m | 35N01 |
| +1950 | 19h 00m | 36N00 |

Note: -4000 = 4001 B.C.
0 = 1 B.C.
+1000 = 1000 A.D.

It will be observed from this table that, for the millennium before the beginning of the Christian era when the development of astrology was at its greatest, the declination of the solar apex was about 35 degrees north, and hence, it passed daily over the zenith in the same geographical parallel of north latitude. If a map of the world is examined, it will be found that this parallel of latitude passes overhead at the Pillars of Hercules, Barbary Coast, Crete, Cypress, just south of the island of Rhodes (where Hipparchus made his observations), north of Egypt, right through Babylonia, Assyria, Persia and Kashmir; in fact through all those countries where astronomy and astrology were born, nurtured and highly developed.

About January 14 (the date advances one full day in 72 years), the Sun is in ecliptic conjunction with its own apex, and simultaneously it enters the constellation Capricorn. Known as the Capsolar, this is the master and most important ingress in the year. This is when Earth is heliocentrically in 0 Cancer. But as the apex does not lie in the plane of the ecliptic (it is 58°04′ north of it), the sun, Earth and apex can never be in alignment. In other words, the sun can never "eclipse" the apex. The date on which the sun is ecliptically in conjunction with the antapex is July 16. At this juncture the point is diametrically in opposition to the apex, and heliocentrically the Earth is in ecliptic conjunction with the apex. Simultaneously the sun enters the constellation Cancer—this is known as the Cansolar ingress. The inference therefore is that the ecliptic longitudes of the solar apex determined 0 Capricorn (of the original Egypto-Babylonian zodiac) and the rest of the zodiacal constellations, each rigourously 30 degrees in extent, were reckoned from this point, thus placing to all intents and purposes permanently the Pleiades in 5 Taurus, Aldebaran in 15 Taurus, Regulus in 5 Leo, Spica in 29 Virgo and Antares in 15 Scorpio.

Incidentally it should be borne in mind that the ancient Egyptian and Babylonian zodiacal constellations were always *exactly* 30 degrees in length. This is proved from monumental records, Babylonian almanacs, lunar and star tables, and Egyptian and Babylonian ephemerides. When Cleostratus of Tenedos imported the zodiac into Greece in the middle of the 6th century B.C., he evidently tried to make the zodiacal symbols conform to the patterns formed in the sky by the groupings of the fixed stars, thereby causing some of the zodiacal constellations to have fewer than 30 degrees and others more than 30 degrees, i.e., Cancer and Leo, but the Egyptians never made this mistake. To them the zodiacal symbols were only hieroglyphic ideograms, and homonyms or rebuses were often substituted for them.

Thus the symbol of the "lion" was only a rebus for a "sickle," both having phonetically the same sound, the sickle being apparently the original symbol for the constellation Leo. During different dynastic periods, varying zodiacal symbols appear. Thus the "two turtles" and "scarabaeus" symbolised Cancer; the "serpent," Scorpio; the "sun on the eastern horizon," Libra; a "fleece," Aries; and a "phallus," Taurus. Leo was also often symbolised by a "knife," as was the planet Mars.

Notwithstanding the fact that the Babylonians produced some of the greatest astronomers of all time, such as Naburiannu (500 B.C.) and Kidinnu (373 B.C.), it seems utterly absurd even to suggest that the ancient astronomers knew of the solar apex and its location, since even with the aid of our generation's marvellous and powerful optical and radio instruments and advanced techniques, its position has not yet been precisely determined. Nor can we bring ourselves to believe that they knew of City-Universes and the like, such discoveries having been made only in very recent times.

Yet how does it come about that 0 Capricorn of the sidereal zodiac tallies so closely and significantly with the mean ecliptic longitude of the apex? Is this merely a coincidence? If so, surely it is a remarkable one. Garth Allen is of the opinion that the ancient star-gazers discovered the "cardinal" points of the zodiac only after many years of patient observation, that is, empirically; and this might well be the case. On the other hand, it is claimed that these Magi were also great magicians versed in all the lore of hypnotism and the like, and capable of inducing and directing a high degree of clairvoyance and clairaudience in the vestal virgins and young boys entranced in the inner sanctum of the temple. Arguing from personal experience, the writer has no doubt but that knowledge, otherwise unobtainable, can be derived by such arcane means. Said Gotama, the Enlightened One:

> "In this fathom-long mortal body the Universe lies hid, I declare. And its cause, and its cessation, and the way that leads to its cessation. On that cessation, *nirvana* is . . ."

# Chapter II

# The Sidereal Zodiac

Astrologers are cognizant of the fact that the *Tetrabiblos* ("Four Books") attributed to Claudius Ptolemy (born in Ptolmais, Egypt; date unknown) and written some time between 100 and 178 A.D., probably about 139 A.D., is the "Bible" of astrology in the western world, even to this day. Most of the astrological rules and aphorisms that have come down to us have been culled directly from it, or are variations of its tenets. The work is addressed by its author to one, Syrus. Who he was, nobody seems to know. At the time the *Tetrabiblos* was written, astrology had been flourishing in Greece, Rome and the Hellenistic world for several centuries, and prior to Ptolemy there were quite a few Greek and Roman astrological authors, such as Vettius Valens, author of the *Anthology,* Manetho (born May 28, 80 AD); author of the *Apotelesmatica,* Bilbillus, Antigonus of Nicaea, Aristides and Criodemus, to say nothing of the legendary Petosiris and Nechepso; while in Rome we find Manitius penning his *Astronomicon* during the reign of the Emperor Tiberius. Ptolemy informs us in his *Tetrabiblos* (1,10):

> "For this reason, although there is no natural beginning to the zodiac, since it is a circle, *they* assume that the sign that begins with the vernal equinox is the starting point of all."[1]

The *they* in this quotation appears to refer to Posidonius of Apameia and his school who, according to Bouche-Leclerq, were the first to invent the modern version of the tropical zodiac with the vernal equinoctial point permanently fixed at the beginning of Aries in 0 Aries. A pupil of Hipparchus, Posidonius appears to have been born about 130 B.C., dying about 51 B.C. A Stoic philosopher and authority on astrological ethnology, he is credited with being a great traveller and author of some 50 works covering a wide range of scientific subjects; and he numbered among his pupils Geminus and Cicero. Hipparchus' tractate, *Concerning the*

---

[1] The edition quoted from is "Ptolemy, *Tetrabiblos,* edited and translated into English by F. E. Robbins, Ph.D., University of Michigan, U.S.A." Harvard University Press, MCMXL, Loeb Classical Library.

*Shifting (Metaptosis) of the Tropical and Equinoctial Points*—now lost—has been discussed by Ptolemy in his *Almagest* ("Great Work"), Book 2, Chapter 2, and Book 7, Chapters 1, 2 and 3. Many astronomers, for instance Montuela, Bailly, Delambre, Vince, Woodhouse, Whewell, Martin, Ball, Newcomb, Young and Berry, took the title of the tractate literally, namely that Hipparchus actually discovered the retrogression of the equinoxes. But others, such as Ptolemy himself, Copernicus, Riccioli, Gregory, Weidler, Laplace, Lalande, Long, Rothman, Narrien, Arago, Hoefer, Flammarion and Wolf, concluded, notwithstanding the title of the tractate, that both Hipparchus and Ptolemy were firmly convinced that it was the fixed stars that precessed, and not the equinoctial points that regressed; and in a brilliant paper read before the Royal Dublin Society, May 13, 1901, Maxwell Close demonstrated that the latter view was undoubtedly correct. The title of the tractate is no more literally accurate than that of an astronomer who wrote a tractate on "the calculation of the sunrise," whilst knowing full well that the rising of the sun is only apparent, the real motion being the downward rotation of the eastern horizon.

This subject is of the greatest importance in our study of the evolution of the modern zodiac. Because the vernal point *perpetually* rose exactly due east and set exactly due west in what the Greeks termed the eighth, or rotating, sphere, the ancients were convinced and more so after the discovery of the phenomena of precession—that the equinoctial and solstitial points were the only fixed points in the heavens, and hence no zodiac could be valid unless riveted to one of them. And this conviction obtained until Copernicus, in the 17th century, devised what is now known as the Copernican system in contradistinction to the Ptolemaic system, when he discovered that it was the Earth that went around the Sun, not vice versa. In consequence, therefore, it was the equinoctial and solstitial points that were precessing—or rather regressing, and not the fixed stars. That epoch-making discovery sounded the death knell of the tropical system, but few astrologers harkened to its toll.

Although more than two-thirds of some 180 Greek horoscopes surviving to this day antedate Ptolemy's time, and the other third belong to the succeeding couple of centuries, nevertheless hardly one of them was computed in terms of Ptolemy's, or rather Posidonius' zodiac. On the contrary, virtually all were computed in terms of what is now known by scientists as "System A" or "System B." Although originally sidereal, both these zodiacs were tropical. In fact, all Greek zodiacs—and there were many—were tropical. But in System A the vernal point was *fixed* in 10 Aries, whereas in System B it was fixed in 8 Aries. The most popular of all the Greek tropical zodiacs was System B, and according to Professor Otto Neugebauer, it flourished ". . . far into the Middle Ages." Before the inauguration of these systems, there was a tropical zodiac wherein the vernal point was fixed in 12 Aries, and another where the point was fixed in 15 Aries. Achilles Tatius (3rd century A.D.) writes:

> "Some place the tropics in the beginning, others about the

eighth degree, some about the twelfth, and others about the fifteenth." (Isag. 23)

Why so many conflicting tropical zodiacs current in ancient Greece, vying with one another in popularity? How did they come into being? According to J.K. Fotheringham, reader of Ancient Astronomy and Chronology in the University of Oxford, the great event in the development of exact astronomy in Greece was the sending away of a collection of Babylonian observation tablets by Callisthenes at the request of his uncle, Aristotle. Since Babylon fell into Alexander's hands in 331 B.C., and Callisthenes was executed in 327 B.C., the date of this event is known exactly (*Observatory*, October 1928). Among these and other Babylonian tablets, subsequently discovered were soli-lunar tables attributed to the Babylonian astronomer Naburianos (Naburiannu). Here the vernal point was placed in 10 Aries, and the soli-lunar tables, attributed to Cidenas (Kidinnu), show it in 8 Aries. As Naburianos and Cidenas ranked—and still do rank—amongst the greatest astronomers of all time, the Greeks eagerly accepted these tables, devising zodiacs with the vernal equinox point fixed in either 10 or 8 Aries according to whether they favoured Naburianos or Cidenas. It is known that the epoch of Naburianos' tables is 508 B.C. at which time the vernal equinox point was actually in 10 Aries of the sidereal or fixed zodiac (about to be discussed), and the epoch of Cidenas' tables was 373 B.C., at which date the sidereal longitude of the vernal point was actually in 8 Aries. Firmly believing that the vernal equinox point was fixed absolutely in the heavens, Greek astronomers were confronted with a problem, for Naburianos and Cidenas could not, in their opinion, both be right. The majority of Greek astronomers and astrologers favoured Cidenas' evaluation, that is System B with the vernal point fixed absolutely in 8 Aries. This was the tropical zodiac of Manetho, Manillius, Firmicus Maternus, Vettius Valens and many others. It is also the system employed in the construction of the famous rectangular and circular zodiacs of the Egypto-Roman temple at Denderah, and calculated for April 17, 17 A.D.

Towards the end of the 19th and beginning of the 20th centuries, a great collection of Babylonian cuneiform tablets was excavated from the magnificent astrological library of Ashur-bani-pal (668-626 B.C.) at Nineveh, while many more were found elsewhere in Mesopotamia. These included observation tablets, prediction tablets, lunar tablets, Jupiter tablets, fixed star tablets, Babylonian almanacs, Babylonian ephemerides, and the like, many of them going back to the third millennia B.C. These were critically examined by such internationally known scholars and scientists as Epping, Kugler, Weidner, Schaumberger, Rehm, Schoch, Neugebauer, Sachs, Van der Waerden and many others. Indeed, the literature on this subject is considerable and can only be lightly touched upon here. They discovered that the longitudes as given in these tablets were not reckoned from the equinoxes or solstices. In other words, they were not tropical, but were reckoned from the fixed stars.

Therefore, the zodiac of the ancient Babylonians, and also that of the Egyptians—for the Demotic Stabart Tables and the Berlin Papyrus P8279 fall into the same category—were essentially sidereal, or "starry," which means that the zodiac was reckoned from the fixed stars and not from the ever-shifting equinoctial points. When all longitudes were reduced to the epoch 101 B.C. (-100 B.C.), it was found that the mean *ayanamsa* or difference in longitude between the modern tropical and sidereal zodiacs was, for that epoch, 4.3, the standard error of a single observation being 0.6. But with the subsequent discovery of more material, this error has been much reduced. This proves that the Egyptians and Babylonians measured their longitudes from the Pleiades in 5 Taurus, Aldebaran in 15 Taurus, Regulus in 5 Leo, Spica in 29 Virgo, and Antares in 15 Scorpio, such marking stars being known as "fiducials."

Astronomers are high in their praise of the astonishing accuracy of the Babylonian tablets and computations.

> "I can say of the Babylonians, who were persistent observers of the crescent during 3,000 years, that not only their observations, but also their computations for ephemerides are admirable." (Carl Schoch, *Venus Tablets of Ammizaduga*)

Others say much the same thing. Yet their calculations of the equinoxes and solstices were frequently as much as five days in error! (See O. Neugebauer's "A Table of Solstices from Uruk," *Journal of Cuneiform Studies*, 1, 1947. The reason for this was that, unlike the Greeks who placed great importance on the accurate determination of their dates, the Babylonians considered time estimates of secondary importance, merely using them to determine the length of daylight, where an approximate figure could suffice. This fact alone proves that the Babylonian zodiac could not possibly have been tropical.

Proof that the Babylonian zodiac was the original *astrological* zodiac was established on May 14, 1949, when the mystery of the origin of the traditional exaltation degrees of the planets in the zodiac *(hypsomata)* was solved. These figures proved to be the *sidereal* longitudes of the planets at their heliacal risings and settings for the lunar year 786 B.C., the mean value of the *ayanamsa* being 14.5 degrees. This, reduced to the epoch -100 (101 B.C.), equated to 4.6 degrees, thereby agreeing with what was determined from the Babylonian and Egyptian records. (See C. Fagan's *Zodiacs, Old and New,* 1950, and "The Astrologer's Zodiac," *In Search*, Fall 1959). The fact that the *ayanamsa* for the *hypsomata* agreed with that from these ancient records sets the seal of authenticity on its discovery.

Although the oldest extant horoscope in the world is of the inauguration of the Sothic Era, July 16, 2767 B.C. at Heliopolis, Egypt, at the heliacal rising of Sirius (see Fagan's *The Symbolism of the Constellations,* Moray Series No. 6, page 45 et seq.), which was in terms of the sidereal zodiac, the oldest extant genethliacal horoscopes are six Babylonian genitures examined by Professor A. Sachs, Brown University, Providence, Rhode Island. (see "Babylonian Horoscopes," *Journal of Cuneiform Studies*, Vol. VI, No. 2). The earliest of these six horoscopes is dated April 29, 410 B.C. and the latest is March 1, 142 B.C. When compared with computations from modern tables, it was found that the longitudes of the planets, where recorded, were in terms of the sideral zodiac (see *American Astrology*, January 1956). Incidentally, the earliest extant Greek "horoscope" is for the coronation of Antiochus I of Commagene. This takes the form of a colossal relief of a lion on the summit of Nimrod Dagh, 7,000 feet above sea level in the Taurus range. Besides the 19 fixed stars of Leo, there are also depicted on the lion a grouping of the Moon, Jupiter, Mercury and Mars. Professor Otto Neugebauer shows that such a grouping tallied with July 7, 62 B.C., when a quadruple conjunction of Jupiter, Mars, Mercury and the Moon took place in Leo, according to:

". . . the Eudoxean or Mesopotamian (Babylonian) norms for the sign Leo." (See O. Neugebauer and H. B. Van Hoesen's *Greek Horoscopes,* 1959)

Having regard to the locality, we may have little hesitation in believing it was the latter.

It will be helpful to give here the mean sidereal longitude of the vernal point for the following centuries:

| *Year* | *Aries* |
|---|---|
| -100 | 4° 27' |
| 0 | 3° 04' |
| 100 A.D. | 1° 41' |
| 200 A.D. | 0° 18' |

Scholars estimate that the *Almagest* and *Tetrabiblos* were written some time about 139 A.D., at which period the mean sidereal longitude of the vernal point was 1 Aries 09. But Vogt determined the longitude of Ptolemy's vernal point to be in error by 1° 15' (See H. Vogt's *Versuch einer Widerherstellung von Hipparchs Fixsternverzeichnis,* 1925). This means that, when the *Tetrabiblos* was written, there was only an insignificant difference of -0° 06' between the sidereal and Ptolemy's zodiac. So, to all intents and purposes, the zodiac of the *Tetrabibios* is sidereal throughout! Many chapters can be cited in support of this statement, such as II, 3; II, 7; III, 16; IV, 5; IV, 9, where the zodiacal and outer constellations are considered together. Ptolemy speaks of the effects of ". . . the hinder parts of Aries and Leo, the Pitcher, the face of Capricorn, the Gorgon's head in Perseus, Cepheus, and Andromeda," etc. As these star clusters have now moved, owing to precession, far from the position they occupied in the tropical zodiac of Ptolemy's day, it is manifest that this ancient astronomer never contemplated such an eventuality, otherwise he would have given instructions for their future location. In short, he was thinking only in terms of the sidereal zodiac.

There is one passage in particular which brings this home to us. He says the system of houses is of the following nature.

> "Since of the twelve signs the most northern—closer than the others to our zenith and, therefore, more productive of heat and warmth—are Cancer and Leo. They *assigned* these to the greatest and most powerful of the heavenly bodies, i.e., to the luminaries, as 'houses'; Leo, which is masculine, to the Sun, and Cancer, feminine, to the Moon."
> *(Tetrabiblos,* I, 17)

Back in the tropical zodiac, the signs Cancer and Leo, taken as a pair, were never the most northern of the twelve signs, or closest to our zenith; nor are they now. In our hemishpere, the Sun is the most northern and the nearest to the zenith when in 30 Gemini or 0 Cancer—which is saying the same thing. Hence, in the tropical zodiac Gemini and Cancer are the most northerly of the twelve signs, and thus they will always be in that zodiac. Ptolemy was far too great an astronomer to make such a mistake as this; he could not possibly have been referring to the tropical zodiac at all. In fact, it is doubtful whether he knew of such a zodiac, notwithstanding his statement that the zodiac commenced with the vernal equinox in Aries, especially so as, during this time, the sidereal zodiac *also* commenced with the vernal equinox at the beginning of Aries. So we must conclude that, if not referring to the tropical zodiac, he must have meant the sidereal one. In the sidereal zodiac, Cancer and Leo *were* the most northerly of the twelve and nearest to the zenith about 1955 B.C.—the beginning of the Arian Age, the time when the summer solstice occurred with the Sun in the last degree of the constellation Cancer, or at the beginning of the first degree of the constellation Leo. In this connection it will be noticed that Ptolemy specifically states "they assigned. " But he does not inform us who "they" were. "They" could not have been Hipparchus, Posidonius or Geminus, as these astronomers were of the late period. Nor could they have been the shadowy Nechepso and Petosiris, ascribed by scholars to the 5th or 4th century BC. "They" therefore, must have been the astrologers who flourished about the 2nd millennium B.C. which inference would also afford a clue as to the date of the formation of the rulerships in connection with the twelve zodiacal constellations, unless of course the rulership scheme was devised in retrospect.

It seems quite evident from the copious evidence before us that Claudius Ptolemy was a sidereal astrologer, and that the *Tetrabiblos* was a text book on sidereal astrology. It was a tragedy of great magnitude that his words as to the beginning of the zodiac should, inevitably have been misunderstood in the succeeding centuries. The *Almagest* and *Tetrabiblos* are the sole authorities for the modern tropical zodiac; now, alas, the standard zodiac of the western world.

To enable the reader to rectify this unfortunate misinterpretation by eliminating all precession that has accrued since the "zero year" 221 A.D., and restore the zodiacal signs to their rightful places amongst the fixed stars is the purpose of the calculations incorporated in this primer. Many astrologers have independently discovered that the dating of transits can be proved accurate only when the precession that has accrued from the date of the radix has been expunged. But this is a partial and mathematically objectionable practice, as the tropical zodiac is inherently precessional; to suffer any such expurgation, even in part, is inadmissable. What is more, such expurgations become totally unnecessary when operating in the ex-precessional sidereal zodiac. It is, however, in the calculation of the solar and lunar returns, or revolutions, that the effects of precession become apparent. For instance, when a calculation is made in respect of a man of sixty years, the difference in time between the return of the Sun to the place it occupied at his birth in the tropical and sidereal zodiacs can amount to nearly twenty-one hours, with a consequent difference in the longitude of the Moon and the house positions of the planets. To a lesser extent the same is equally true of the difference in time between the sidereal and tropical lunar returns.

It was during 1957 that Garth Allen, the brilliant astrologer and amateur astronomer of the U.S.A., experimenting with solar and lunar ingresses into the sidereal "cardinal" constellations, discovered that these charts, in a most astonishing and convincing way, accounted for most of the great calamities that had occurred during their operation: earthquakes, explosions, fires, accidents, shipwrecks, etc. But, when progressed for the dates of the calamities, all were found by him to be slightly out, the mean error being equivalent to an increase of $0°\ 06'\ 05''$ in the then-adopted sidereal longitude of the vernal point, determined from Spica in 29 Virgo, and the proper motion having been allowed for. In short, for the epoch 1950.0 he proposed as the mean longitude of the vernal point $335°\ 57'\ 28.64''$, proper motion being disregarded. This new fiducial point was termed by him "The Synetic Vernal Point" (S.V.P.), and this has since been adopted by siderealists (see *American Astrology*, May 1957).

## Chapter III

# Converson of a Tropical Map into the Sidereal

The vast majority of horoscopes calculated in the Western world are in terms of the modern version of the tropical zodiac. Hipparchus, when compiling his star catalogue, plotted the positions of the fixed stars from the equinoctial and solstitial points for the year 139 B.C. approximately, and Posidonius apparently improved on this idea by making the zodiac as a whole commence with the vernal point fixed in 0 Aries. This, then, was the birth of the modern version of the tropical zodiac. Before Hipparchus' time it had no existence, and it was entirely a Greek innovation.

As already pointed out, at the time the *Tetrabiblos* was written the vernal point had retrograded to the beginning of the ancient Egypto-Babylonian fixed zodiac, so Claudius Ptolemy, very naturally and quite correctly for the time in which he lived, i.e., the 2nd century A.D., stated that the zodiac commenced with the equinoctial point. Unfortunately, his followers and translators, not understanding the real situation, took Ptolemy's statement on its face value and they thus caused Posidonius' tropical zodiac to become the more popular.

The tropical zodiac begins with the vernal (spring) equinoctial point which retrogrades along the circular path of the ecliptic at the rate of one degree of longitude in about 71.5 years. As the spring point is retrograding, so also is the tropical zodiac as a whole. This movement is known as the precession (or more correctly "the regression") of the equinoxes. Consequently the tropical zodiac has been styled the "moving zodiac," because it is perpetually moving against the order of the zodiacal constellations. It is also recognized as the precessional zodiac. On the other hand, the sidereal "starry" zodiac, which, from remote times had been the zodiac of Egypt, Babylonia, Assyria and the Chaldeans, is to all intents and purposes riveted to the fixed stars and, consequently, is non-moving and hence nonprecessional.

It was about the middle of the year 221 A.D. when the tropical zodiac had retrograded to the precise conjunction with its sidereal counterpart, both zodiacs thereby tallying, i.e., there was no difference between them. But since that "zero year," the tropical zodiac has continued to shift backwards in respect of the fixed stars, so that by the beginning of 1963 A.D. the divergence between them will amount to 24°13′10″. This divergence, or difference between the commencements of the two zodiacs is technically known by the Sanskrit word *ayanamsa*. Longitudes of the Sun, Moon, planets and fixed stars, etc., in the tropical zodiac are known as tropical longitudes, whereas those in the sidereal zodiac are known as sidereal longitudes. The *ayanamsa* for a given date is found by subtracting the sidereal longitude of the vernal point (here styled the "Synetic Vernal Point" or S.V.P.) for the same date, from 360 degrees.

Incidentally, it should be remembered that the tropical longitude of the S.V.P. is always in 0 Aries. From the year 221 A.D. onwards, the *ayanamsa* can be found simply by subtracting the numerical value of the S.V.P. from 30 degrees. For 0 hours U.T. on January 1, 1963, the sidereal longitude of the S.V.P. is Pisces 5° 46' 49.62". Let us deduct this from 30 degrees:

```
                    30 00 00.00
                   -05 46 49.62
       ayanamsa =   24 13 10.38
```

To ascertain a sidereal longitude, simply subtract the *ayanamsa* from the tropical longitude. Thus, a tropical ephemeris for 1963 gives the Sun's longitude at 0 hours U.T. on January 1, 1963, as 8° Capricorn 49′ 21″. We will now find the sidereal equivalent:

| | | |
|---|---|---|
| Sun's tropical longitude | Capricorn | 08 49 21 |
| Subtract *ayanamsa* for January 1, 1963 | | 24 13 10 |
| | Sagittarius | 14 36 11 |

A quicker way is to add the numerical value of the S.V.P. and mentally deduct one sign (30 degrees).

| | | |
|---|---|---|
| Sun's tropical longitude | Capricorn | 08 49 21 |
| Add S.V.P. | | 05 46 50 |
| Deducting one sign | Sagittarius | 14 36 11 |

N.B. We have omitted here decimals of a second.

The S.V.P. can be found in many tropical ephemerides. In order to convert a tropical into a sidereal horoscope, the *ayanamsa* for the date of the horoscope must be deducted from ALL tropical longitudes, including the cusps of the twelve houses. As precession is always negative, it follows that in subtracting the *ayanamsa* or adding the S.V.P., one is actually expunging from the tropical horoscope all the precession that has accrued since A.D. 221.

## Chapter IV

# The Mean Sun (M.S.)

One of the most important factors in the calculation of the progressed and regressed horoscopes, and the quotidian or daily charts, is the right ascension of the *Mean* Sun, or, as abbreviated, the "M.S." As textbooks in general say nothing about it, a few words would seem necessary here. The *Mean* Sun is purely fictitious. It has no more reality than the *mean* longitude of the Moon's ascending node (caput draconis) given in virtually all astrological tropical and sidereal ephemerides. When the appropriate equations are applied to them, their *true* longitudes can be ascertained and the true longitude of the node can exceed its mean longitude by almost plus or minus two degrees.

The "sidereal time" at noon as given in Raphael's ephemerides is the "M.S." expressed in time for Greenwich mean noon, or 12 hours U.T. It increases at the constant rate of 9.855 seconds per hour, so that by midnight it will have increased by 1m 58.278s. In midnight ephemerides, wherein the sidereal time is tabulated for 0 hours U.T., the tabulated sidereal time (plus or minus 12 hours) is the M.S. for 0 hours U.T. It, too, increases at the rate of 9.856 seconds per hour. For the purposes of calculation only, the M.S. can be treated as if it were a planet with a constant daily motion of 3m 56.556s (diurnal log 0.78443). The student will be spared a lot of confusion and irritating mistakes in calculation if he ignores "a.m." and "p.m." in his computations, and thinks always in terms of a 24-hour clock. Noon ephemerides always used and still use astronomical time (A.T.), i.e., time in terms of a 24-hour clock commencing at Greenwich mean noon, so that 9:00 p.m. on March 31 = 900 A.T. March 31. But 9:00 a.m. G.M.T. on April 1 = 2100 A.T. March 31. In medieval times up to the middle of the 18th century, all horoscopes were computed in astronomical time, the day being held to commence at noon. On the other hand, the midnight ephemerides conform to the 24-hour clock now in common use in the scientific and commercial world, and known as universal time (U.T.). Thus 9:00 a.m. G.M.T. = 900 U.T. whilst 9:00 p.m. G.M.T. = 2100 U.T. on the same day. Students should always remember that Raphael's ephemerides continue to use the now obsolete astronomical time.

When calculating the M.S., instead of resorting to diurnal logs, the following simple rule will enable the increase in the M.S. known as "acceleration," to be found as follows:

Rule: To the tabulated sidereal time or equinoctial time, which is the same thing, on the required date, for every hour of A.T. or U.T., as the case may be, add 10 seconds, and for every 6 minutes add 1 second. Then from their sum deduct one second if the time exceeds 6 hours, 2 seconds if it exceeds 12 hours, and 3 seconds if it exceeds 18 hours.

Example 1: Given *Raphael's Ephemeris for 1961*, find the M.S. for 4:15 p.m. July 6, 1961. As G.M.T. is five hours east of E.S.T., the equivalent G.M.T. will be 9:15 p.m., which equals 915 A.T., as this is a noon ephemeris.

|  | H M S |
|---|---|
| A.T. 915 Acceleration for 9 hours | 00 01 30 |
| Acceleration for 15 minutes | 02 |
| Sidereal time at noon | 06 56 55 |
|  | 06 58 27 |
| As 9:15 exceeds 6 hours, deduct | 01 |
| Required M.S. | 0658 26 |

Example 2: Find the M.S. for 4:15 a.m. E.S.T. on July 7, 1961. The equivalent G.M.T. will be 9:15 a.m. = 2115 A.T. on July 6 (not 7), 1961.

|  | H M S |
|---|---|
| A.T. 2115 Acceleration for 21 hours | 00 03 30 |
| Acceleration for 15 minutes | 02 |
| Sidereal time at noon on July 6 | 06 56 55 |
|  | 07 00 27 |
| As 21 hours A.T. exceeds 18 hours, deduct | 03 |
| Required M.S. | 07 00 24 |

Example 3: Find the M.S. for 915 U.T. July 7,1961. Using a midnight ephemeris, the tabulated equinoctial time, a more appropriate term for sidereal time, must be increased or diminished by 12 hours.

|  | H M S |
|---|---|
| U.T. 915 Acceleration for 9 hours | 00 01 30 |
| Acceleration 15 minutes | 02 |
| Equinoctial time | 18 58 53 |
|  | 19 00 25 |
| Less 12 hrs and 1 sec, as 9:15 exceeds 6 hrs | 12 00 01 |
| Required M.S. | 07 00 24 |

# Chapter V

# The Calendar

Notwithstanding the reforms of Julius Caesar in 45 B.C. and Pope Gregory XIII in the year 1582 A.D., our calendar remains a clumsy and anachronistic contraption, having no place in this modern world. It is, if fact, another variation of the tropical zodiac—the zodiacal signs being months of unequal length. In its ideal prototype this tropical calendar commenced at "Spring Day," with the vernal point fixed on March 1, the first day of the year, with leap-year day, when it occurred, being placed at the end of February, the last day of the year. But today we find the calendar so much out of gear with its prototype that the year commences on January 1. Leap-year day is stuck at the end of the second month and the vernal equinox point is *fixed* on March 21. All this, in the light of astronomy, is absurd, and it occasions many unnecessary complications in computations. If error is to be avoided, it is advisable for the modern astrologer to abandon the Gregorian calendar and commence the year again with March 1 and then reckon all dates, not in terms of months, but as days of the year commencing with March 1. The following table will enable the reader to effect the change at sight.

**The Astronomical Year**

|         |       | *Day* |           |       | *Day* |
|---------|-------|-----|-----------|-------|-----|
| March   | 0 =   | 0   | September | 0 =   | 184 |
| April   | 0 =   | 31  | October   | 0 =   | 214 |
| May     | 0 =   | 61  | November  | 0 =   | 245 |
| June    | 0 =   | 92  | December  | 0 =   | 275 |
| July    | 0 =   | 122 | January   | 0 =   | 306 |
| August  | 0 =   | 153 | February  | 0 =   | 337 |

Example 1: What is the equivalent astronomical date for May 12, 1895? May 0 in the table is given as 61; then 61 + 12 = 73. Hence the astronomical date is 1895, the 73rd day.

Example 2: What is the equivalent astronomical date for February 14, 1961? February 0 =

337 + 14 = 351, so, therefore, the astronomical date is 1960, the 351st day. It should be noted here that as the year commences on March 1, January and February are considered as belonging to the previous year, in this case 1960.

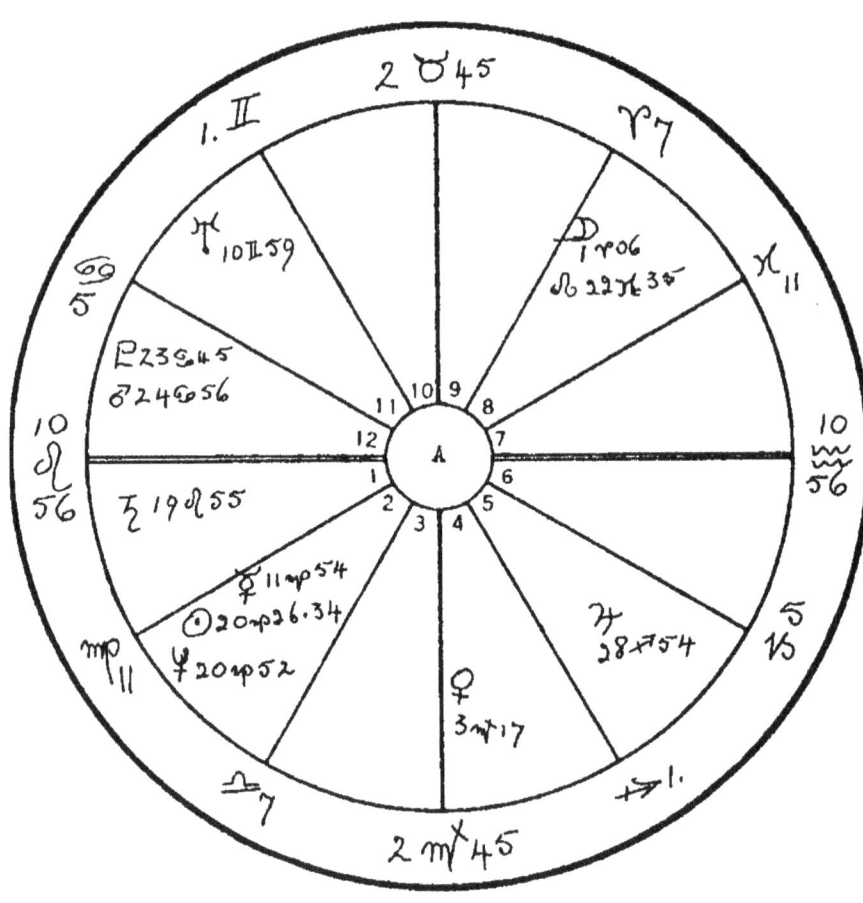

*Map A*
*Susan Walker, October 8, 1949 2:33 a.m. GMT, London, 0W10 51N30*

## Chapter VI

# The Example Horoscope

In this edition of the *Primer of Sidereal Astrology* we have decided not to deal with the maps of kings, queens or presidents in order to demonstrate the different sidereal methods to be shown in the *Primer,* but to use that of one which we can feel certain was accurately timed, a necessity for accurate work in any zodiac. It may be that we could have chosen individual maps for each method which would have shown a greater closeness to the angles, but by choosing this one map for all our methods we clear ourselves of any possible charge that our maps are specifically picked for a purpose.

The map chosen, given as Map A on the opposite page, is that of Brigadier Firebrace's granddaughter, Susan Walker. The requisite "important event" in her young life was provided by a serious accident which took place on March 27, 1960, at about 12 noon G.M.T. at Blewbury, Berkshire, England, longitude 1W17, latitude 51N35. Susan, then aged 10, was thrown from her pony, being rendered unconscious and sustaining a cracked skull. We are happy to say that she has made a complete recovery.

Susan was born in Kensington, London (0W09.44, 51N29.33), on October 8, 1949 at 2:33 a.m. G.M.T. At her grandfather's request, the time of birth was carefully observed by the doctor and the nurse and is certainly not subject to any considerable rectification.

We will here admit that as astrologers we are uncertain what constitutes the astrological time of birth. There may even be an astrological time of birth which does not coincide with any physical event. We leave this question open but refer to it as from certain of the maps to be shown we are confident that the fingers of the rectifiers will be itching to advance the time of birth by some eight minutes. We ourselves, however, prefer to work from the unrectified time.

Now we will calculate this map using a noon ephemeris for 1949.

|                                 | H M S    |
|---------------------------------|----------|
| Time from previous noon, Oct 7  | 14 33    |
| Acceleration                    | 02 24    |
| Sidereal time, noon Oct 7       | 13 03 12 |
| Sidereal time, Greenwich        | 03 38 36 |
| Birthplace West of Greenwich    | 39       |
| Sidereal time of birth          | 03 37 57 |

## The Calculation of the Position of the Sun

As it is essential for sidereal calculations to obtain the exact position of the Sun and to a lesser degree that of the Moon, we will show how these can be calculated using ternary and diurnal logarithms as given in *Sidereal Calculation Tables*. Calculating the Sun:

|                              | H M S    |                    |
|------------------------------|----------|--------------------|
| Time from noon               | 14 33    | Diurnal log .21735 |
| Sun's motion Oct 7/8         | 59 13    | Ternary log .48283 |
| Add ternary antilog 35m 54s  |          | .70018             |
| Sun at noon, Oct 7           | 13 52 54 | Libra              |
| Add increment                | 35 54    |                    |
|                              |          |                    |
| Birth Sun tropical zodiac    | 14 28 48 | Libra              |
| To convert, add S.V.P.       | 05 57 46 |                    |
| Birth Sun sidereal zodiac    | 20 26 34 | Virgo              |

## The Calculation of the Position of the Moon

Owing to the speed of the Moon and its varying motion it is not necessary to use the above method for its calculation. We can content ourselves with the use of diurnal logarithms.

|                          | H M    |                        |
|--------------------------|--------|------------------------|
| Time from Noon, Oct 7    | 14 33  | Diurnal log .21735     |
| Moon's motion, Oct 7/8   | 11 48  | .30833                 |
| Add diurnal antilog      | 07 08  | .52568                 |
|                          |        |                        |
| Moon, noon Oct 7         | 17 59  |                        |
| Add increment            | 07 08  |                        |
|                          | 25 07  | Aries (tropical zodiac)|
| Add S.V.P.               | 05 58  |                        |
|                          | 01 05  | Aries (sidereal zodiac)|

# Chapter VII

# The Progressed Horoscope

During the last few centuries, mathematicians amongst astrologers have from time to time invented many new systems of primary interplanetary directing. These have had their day and ceased to be. In this book we will only deal with the primary directing of angles (Chapter VIII), which we believe to be valid and important.

The old fashioned system of progression still holds sway. Rightly used it is the main source of prediction and has given astonishing results; for this reason it is still deservedly popular. Attributed to the Arabs, it is styled the "secondary system of directing" to distinguish it from the "primary system" devised by Claudius Ptolemy, which long ago went out of fashion. In astrological language, the secondary system seeks to interpret the ancient legend that states:

> "A year is as a day in the sight of the Lord."

In other words, to give an example, should the Sun form an exact opposition to Jupiter 20 days after the birth of the native, then, knowing this, the astrologer could predict with every assurance of being justified in time that in his twenty-first year the native would prosper and be joyous of heart. In schools and universities he would win honours. Or should he be of the religious type, he would experience a deep illumination which would colour the rest of his life. On the other hand, if the Sun should be in opposition to Saturn the native would be a failure in that year and suffer one of the bitterest disappointments of his life. Unfortunately, even this system is beginning to lose favour. Why? In the first place because too much is expected of it, astrologers thinking that it should presage all events of life, whereas it can only embrace the "incidents" (accidents being indicated by transits and transit charts). Secondly, very few know how to compute progressions correctly, irrespective of the zodiac used.

**The Two Fundamental Errors**

1. In the secondary system it is held that, as each day after birth is equivalent to one year of life, it only appears necessary to calculate a horoscope for the time of birth for every day af-

ter birth to obtain the equivalent progressed horoscope. In doing this it is assumed that the R.A.M.C. advances at a constant rate of 0h 3m 57s per day after birth, i.e., that the M.C. increases at the approximate rate of one degree per year of life.

This is a fundamental error because its true progress is 24h 03m 57s per day, Earth making one complete revolution on its axis in respect of the fixed stars. At first sight an astrologer would say that 0h 03m 57s seems to be the same as 24h 03m 57s. But is it? Suppose it were necessary to calculate the progressed horoscope when the native was just six months old. By how much would the R.A.M.C. have advanced—0h 01m 58s or 12h 01m 58s? What would be the position of Earth and hence Midheaven and Ascendant in respect of the fixed stars? Obviously it would only have half revolved and therefore the progress for six months would be 12h 01m 58s. It follows that the true rate of progress of the R.A.M.C. is 24h 03m 57s per year. It is on this true and remarkable fact that the "Quotidian" or Daily Chart is based.

2. To elucidate the second fundamental error, we will take an example. Suppose that a native is born at noon G.M.T. on August 1, 1900, and that it is desired to compute his progressed horoscope for his thirtieth birthday, which would naturally fall on August 1, 1930. The usual method is to count 30 days after birth which would tally with August 31, 1900, and to calculate a horoscope for Greenwich mean noon on that day. This would be taken as his progressed horoscope equivalent to August 1, 1930. Are we not here making his progressed birth date, August 31, 1900, equivalent to August 1, 1930, when the native will not be 30 years old but 30 years less 30 days, reckoning as we should from the progressed date and not from the date of birth? Look at the following short table.

|   | 1900 Aug. | 1 is equivalent to | 1900 Aug. 1 |
|---|---|---|---|
|   | 1900 Aug. | 2 is equivalent to | 1901 Aug. 2 |
|   | 1900 Aug. | 3 is equivalent to | 1902 Aug. 3 |
|   | 1900 Aug. | 4 is equivalent to | 1903 Aug. 4 |
|   | . . . . . . . . . . . . . . . . . . . . . . . . . . . . . . . . . . . . . . . . . . . . . . . |
| and | 1900 Aug. | 31 is equivalent to | 1930 Aug. 31 |

Hence, in terms of progressions, the native's thirtieth birthday would have occurred on August 31 and not on August 1 of that year. It is because of this mistake in calculation that secondary directions, especially of the Moon, are often as much as three months in error, depending on the age of the native. The truth of the above observations has been attested by a probe into the underlying mathematics involved in progressions.

## The BIJA

To correct this error use must be made of what the writer terms the *bija* (a Sanskrit word meaning "correction"). The *bija* for one day or one year of life is 0h 3m 55.91s. The use of the *bija* will be seen in the examples which will be given. In the computation of progressed and regressed horoscopes it is always negative, i.e., subtract time.

For the calculation of the *bija* arc for a defmite number of months and days (see Chapter VIII) in the below table, take two hours to represent one month, and four minutes to represent one day.

## Bija Table

| Year | H | M | S | Hour | M | S | Minutes | S |
|---|---|---|---|---|---|---|---|---|
| 1 | 0 | 03 | 56 | 1 | 0 | 10 | 4 | 1 |
| 2 | 0 | 07 | 52 | 2 | 0 | 20 | 10 | 2 |
| 3 | 0 | 11 | 48 | 3 | 0 | 29 | 16 | 3 |
| 4 | 0 | 15 | 44 | 4 | 0 | 39 | 22 | 4 |
| 5 | 0 | 19 | 40 | 5 | 0 | 49 | 28 | 5 |
| 6 | 0 | 23 | 35 | 6 | 0 | 59 | 34 | 6 |
| 7 | 0 | 27 | 31 | 7 | 0 | 09 | 40 | 7 |
| 8 | 0 | 31 | 27 | 8 | 1 | 19 | 46 | 8 |
| 9 | 0 | 35 | 23 | 9 | 1 | 28 | 52 | 9 |
| 110 | 0 | 39 | 19 | 10 | 1 | 38 | 58 | 10 |
| 11 | 0 | 43 | 15 | 11 | 1 | 48 | | |
| 12 | 0 | 47 | 11 | 12 | 1 | 58 | | |
| 13 | 0 | 51 | 07 | 13 | 2 | 08 | | |
| 14 | 0 | 55 | 03 | 14 | 2 | 18 | | |
| 15 | 0 | 58 | 59 | 15 | 2 | 27 | | |
| 16 | 1 | 02 | 55 | 16 | 2 | 37 | | |
| 17 | 1 | 06 | 50 | 17 | 2 | 47 | | |
| 18 | 1 | 10 | 46 | 18 | 2 | 57 | | |
| 19 | 1 | 14 | 42 | 19 | 3 | 07 | | |
| 20 | 1 | 18 | 38 | 20 | 3 | 17 | | |
| 30 | 1 | 57 | 57 | 21 | 3 | 26 | | |
| 40 | 2 | 37 | 16 | 22 | 3 | 36 | | |
| 50 | 3 | 16 | 36 | 23 | 3 | 46 | | |
| 60 | 3 | 55 | 55 | 24 | 3 | 56 | | |
| 70 | 4 | 35 | 14 | | | | | |
| 80 | 5 | 14 | 33 | | | | | |
| 90 | 5 | 53 | 52 | | | | | |
| 100 | 6 | 33 | 00 | | | | | |

25

VERY IMPORTANT: In Chapter V it was stated that the astronomical year begins on March 1, and that January and February are considered to belong to the previous year. There is, however, an important difference with the M.S. which will be used in the calculation of the Sidereal Natal Quotidian. The year for the M.S. begins when it is zero, i.e., on March 22. The period from January 1 to March 22 of every year must be reckoned as belonging to the previous year. This must be remembered or a mistake of a whole year will be made in the calculation.

**Natal Quotidians**

These secondary or Arabic progressions with the difference which we have explained are known as Natal Quotidians, or N.Q.s. They fully justify the belief of astrologers in the day-for-a-year method. They are not a special sidereal technique but can and should be used with maps cast in the tropical zodiac. When we are working in the sidereal zodiac there is one small difference. In the computation of the Sidereal Natal Quotidian, the accumulated precession between the date of birth and the date of the S.N.Q. must be eliminated. This is easily done by adding to the natal M.S. the correction given in the table below according to the age of the native. This corrected M.S. will also be the M.S. of the current Sidereal Solar Return. The correction for a given age will be added to the natal M.S.

| Year | M | S | Year | M | S | Months | M | S |
|---|---|---|---|---|---|---|---|---|
| 1 | 0 | 03 | 10 | 0 | 34 | 4 | 0 | 01 |
| 2 | 0 | 07 | 20 | 1 | 07 | 10 | 0 | 02 |
| 3 | 0 | 10 | 30 | 1 | 41 | 12 | 0 | 03 |
| 4 | 0 | 13 | 40 | 2 | 14 | | | |
| 5 | 0 | 17 | 50 | 2 | 48 | | | |
| 6 | 0 | 20 | 60 | 3 | 21 | | | |
| 7 | 0 | 23 | 70 | 3 | 55 | | | |
| 8 | 0 | 27 | 80 | 4 | 28 | | | |
| 9 | 0 | 30 | 90 | 5 | 02 | | | |
| 10 | 0 | 34 | 100 | 5 | 35 | | | |

**The Sidereal Natal Quotidian (S.N.Q.)**

We will now calculate for our example horoscope the Sidereal Natal Quotidian (S.N.Q.) to the date of the accident, March 27, 1960. For this purpose we shall use a tropical Raphael ephemeris.

As we are working in the sidereal zodiac we must first calculate from our table the correction to the natal M.S. The age at the time of the accident was 10 years 5 months. From the table we see that this necessitates a correction of plus 35 seconds. The natal M.S. being 13h 05m 36s, the M.S. for the S.N.Q. will be 13h 06m 11s.

|  | D | H M S |
|---|---|---|
| M.S. for date, time of event and year 1960 |  | 00 19 40 |
| Corrected Natal M.S. 1949 |  | 13 06 11 |
| Uncorrected age of native in days, etc. | 10 | 11 13 29 |
| Deduct *bija* correcton |  | 41 10 |
| Native's corrected age | 10 | 10 32 19 |
| Day of year and G.M.T. of birth | 221 | 14 33 |
| Day of S.N.Q., i.e., Oct. 18, 1949 | 232 | 01 05 19 |
| Acceleration |  | 11 |
| Sidereal time, noon, Oct. 18, 1949 |  | 13 46 34 |
| S.T. for Greenwich | = | 14 52 04 |
| Birthplace West of Greenwich | - | 39 |
| Sidereal time of S.N.Q. |  | 14 51 25 |

It is for this sidereal time and for the birthplace that Map B has been calculated. The *bija* correction has been obtained from the Table in this chapter.

In Map B we observe that Uranus is near the Descendant, Mars transits opposite progressed Mars, and Uranus is transiting close to natal Pluto. Students of midpoints will notice that the midpoint of transiting Jupiter and Saturn is exactly conjunct the Ascendant. From these maps the secondary directions in force both to natal and progressed planets can be seen. Here, Sun is separating from the opposition to natal Moon, often a time of crisis in the life.

### The Sidereal Natal Ouotidian Regressed (S.N.Q.R.)

If we have calculated the S.N.Q., the calculation of the regressed S.N.Q. is simple. Instead of adding the native's corrected age to the date of year and time of birth, we subtract. Thus:

|  | D | H M S |
|---|---|---|
| Day of year and G.M.T. of birth | 221 | 14 33 |
| Native's corrected age | 10 | 10 32 19 |
| Day of S.N.Q.R., i.e., Sept. 27, 1949 | 211 | 04 00 41 |
| Acceleration |  | 40 |
| S.T. noon, Sept. 27, 1949 |  | 12 23 47 |
| S.T. for Greenwich |  | 16 25 08 |
| Birthplace West of Greenwich |  | 39 |
| Sidereal time of S.N.Q.R. |  | 16 24 29 |

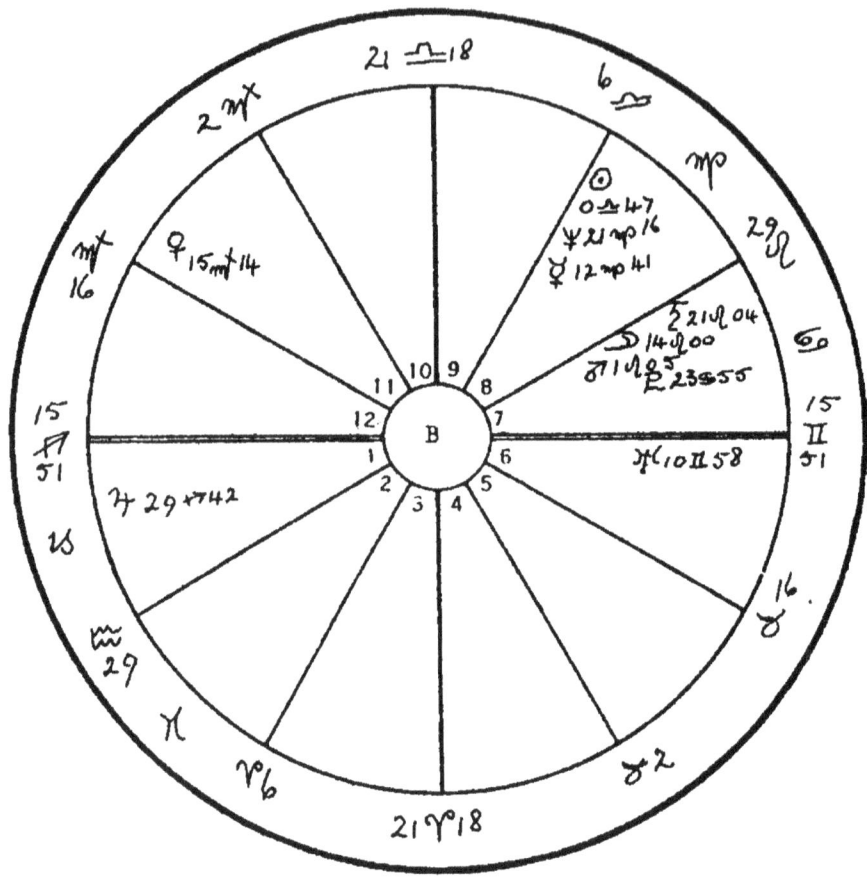

*Map B*
*Susan Walker, Sidereal Natal Quotidian to March 27, 1960*

It is for this sidereal time and for the birthplace that Map C has been erected. Students may, if they so wish, experiment with casting these maps for the place of the event.

We see from Map C that regressed Mars is close to the Descendant, a suitable conjunction. Transiting Uranus is even closer to Pluto than in the S.N.Q. Regressed secondary directions in force are Sun separating from the square of Uranus, and regressed Moon is applying to the square of natal Saturn.

It should again be emphasized that these quotidians are not a special sidereal technique. They may be used with tropical maps when the special correction to the M.S. will not be

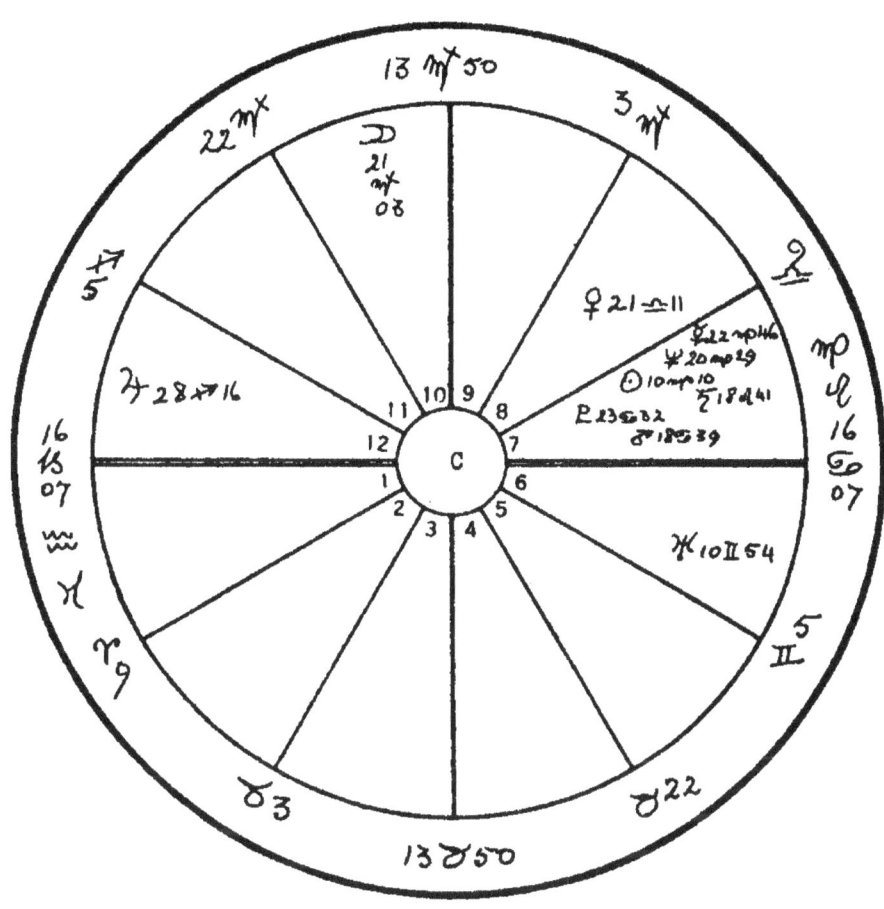

*Map C*
*Susan Walker, Sidereal Natal Quotidian Regressed to March 27, 1960*

necessary. When using a tropical ephemeris all planetary positions must be converted to the sidereal zodiac as explained in Chapter III.

# Chapter VIII

# Primary Directing of the Angles

The primary directing of the angles to the natal planets and to their so-called "second positions" is important. It is, however, only of value when the birth time is known accurately, as an error of about four minutes in time of birth equates to one year of life. It is of great value in the rectification of the horoscope when the time is only approximately known.

Many measures for the advance of the Midheaven have been suggested: one degree, the Naibod rate, the solar arc. We prefer an advance at the so-called *bija* rate, a description of which was given in Chapter VIII. This rate is 3m 55.91s for one year of life.

The Midheaven thus advances regularly by this rate and in so doing makes contact with the natal planets and their second positions. These second positions will differ little from those of the natal planets, as at the age of 60 the advance in time is only some four hours. By then the second position of the Moon will have advanced by some two degrees when computed. This position, which should be taken *in mundo,* is useful for rectification.

Although the angles advance regularly during the year it is convenient to calculate them for the progressed birthday. In a map so obtained, strong contacts with the directed angles will show important trends during the year which could be a background to other maps cast for this period. If we choose the date for this map as the birth day and time, plus the age equated in days—this is the progressed birthday—the calculation is very simple. To show the procedure we will calculate this map for our example horoscope.

| | | |
|---|---|---|
| Birth date and time, Oct. 7, 1949 | 221 days | 14h 33m A.T. |
| Add age, 10 years | <u>10 days</u> | |
| | 231 days | 14h 33m A.T. |

The 231st day is Oct. 17, 1949
We will calculate this map

|  | H | M | S |
|---|---|---|---|
| Date and time (A.T.) Oct. 17, 1949 | 14 | 33 |  |
| Acceleration |  | 02 | 23 |
| Sidereal time, noon, Oct. 17 | 13 | 42 | 38 |
| R.A.M.C. Greenwich | 04 | 18 | 01 |
| Birthplace West of Greenwich |  |  | 39 |
| R.A.M.C. birthplace | 04 | 17 | 22 |

This equates with the equivalent day and month in 1959. By calculating for a date 10 days after the birth date we have eliminated the necessity for considering the *bija* correction. The angles of this map advance at the *bija* rate during the year. If we wish to progress it to a definite date we must add the *bija* increment for the number of months elapsed since October 17 to the sidereal time that we have found. For our event on March 27, 1960, this interval is 170 days 20 hours, or say 5 months 10 days.

From the *bija* table in Chapter VII, take two hours to represent one month and four minutes to represent one day.

|  | M | S |
|---|---|---|
| 5 months (10 hours) | 01 | 38 |
| 10 days (40m) |  | 07 |
| Increment to March 27 | 01 | 45 |

Adding this figure to the S.T. already found for October 17, we arrive at an S.T. of 4h 19m 07s for which time the Map D is drawn. Note that this map is always drawn for the birthplace. This map might tempt an astrologer to rectify it so that Saturn fell directly on the Ascendant. Such a possible rectification must be confmned by other maps. It must be remembered that Susan was for some time under Saturnian restrictions owing to the severe injury.

We do not want to stress the importance of the transits of the minor planets, but we note that Venus accompanied by Mercury transits exactly opposite natal Saturn. It was a Venus (pleasure) Mercury (ride) heavily afflicted by Saturn. In a similar manner a converse map may be drawn by subtracting the same increment from the natal sidereal time. These converse maps are often important.

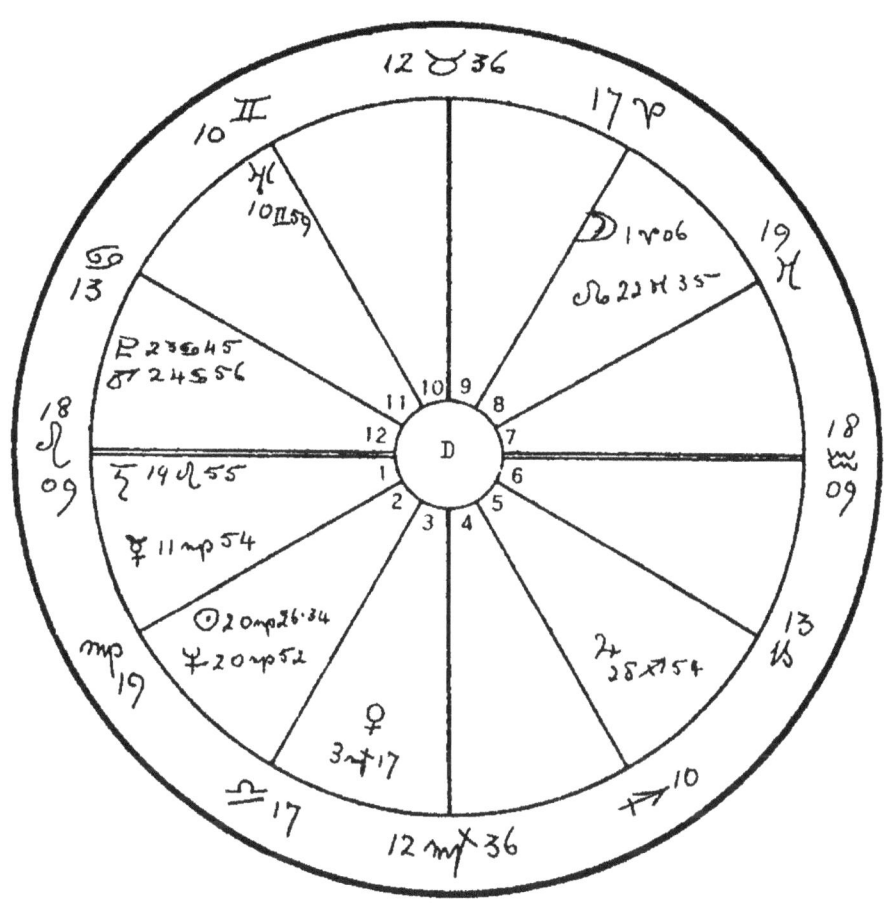

*Map D*
*Susan Walker, Primary Progressed Horoscope to March 27, 1960*

## Chapter IX

# The Sidereal Solar Return (S.S.R.)

One of the oldest methods of astrological prediction is the solar return *a map cast for the exact moment when the Sun each year returns to its birth longitude.* This is in a sense a birthday map, the native being born again yearly. His fortunes during this year are governed by the map of this day. Although still used on the continent it has largely fallen into disrepute amongst British and American astrologers as it has not been found to be reliable. Its sidereal counterpart, which brings the Sun back to its place amongst the fixed stars, is of great value and forms the basis of sound predictive work.

The Sidereal Solar Return (S.S.R.) is not a duplicate of the corresponding tropical return; often the day and always the time will be different. This is due to precession, amounting at the age of 72 to about a full degree. As it is the angles which are the vital and personal part of a solar return, this difference of time is all important. There may be little alteration in longitude in connection with the slower moving planets, but there will be a considerable difference with the Moon.

Until recently there were no sidereal ephemerides. From 1960 onwards they are being published in America. With these ephemerides the calculation of the sidereal solar return is similar to that of the tropical return. The student can use his own technique or he may prefer to use the method outlined below. When no sidereal ephemerides are available, the tropical version can be used. As precession is always negative we have to add it to the tropical longitude of the Sun in order to eliminate it, and then calculate the time of the return of the Sun to this position and not to its natal tropical longitude. In order to get the sidereal time of the return sufficiently accurate we must use at least five-figure logarithms such as those for ternary logarithms given in *Chamber's Mathematical Tables,* or in the special *Sidereal Calculation Tables* of Mary Austin. There is no difficulty in using these table as the procedure is very simple. An example will show the method.

Required: the sidereal time (R.A.M.C.) for the Sidereal Solar Return for 1959 for Susan

Walker. For this calculation we will use a tropical ephemeris giving S.T. for noon. From our example map it will be seen that:

|  |  |  |
|---|---|---|
| Natal sidereal Sun is in | Virgo | 20 26 34 |
| Synetic Vernal Point (Chapter III) |  | 05 57 46 |
| Subtracting and adding one sign, the tropical Sun is in | Libra | 14 28 48 |

For use with our solar return we must annul precession by adding it to this tropical position. The difference between precession at birth and precession of the date of the return is:

| Birth precession | 05 57 46 |
|---|---|
| Precession Oct. 8, 1959 | 05 49 17 |
| Subtracting | 08 29 |

Adding this figure to the natal tropical Sun we obtain 14° Libra 37′ 17″ as the figure we must use in our calculation of our sidereal solar return.

A simpler method is to work from the sidereal Sun and to deduct the synetic vernal point (S.V.P.) for the day of the return. Thus:

| Sidereal Sun | 20 26 34 | Virgo |
|---|---|---|
| S.V.P. Oct. 8, 1959 | 05 49 17 |  |
| Subtract and advance one sign | 14 37 17 | Libra |

It will be seen that we have obtained the same figure as before.

The Synetic Vernal Point is available in most ephemerides, and we give in the appendix a table from which the S.V.P. can be calculated. Based on an approximate rate of 50 minutes per year we can estimate the accrued precession by multiplying the age by ten and dividing the result by twelve. Using this makeshift we would obtain 8′ 20″, but in later life the difference can be much greater and lead to an error on the Midheaven of several degrees.

The tropical longitude which we are now to use restores the Sun to its natal position amongst the fixed stars. Our problem is to calculate the date and time when the Sun reaches tropical 14° Libra 37′ 17″. Our 1959 ephemeris shows that this takes place on October 8, 1959.

There are many methods which can be used for our calculation. We recommend the following for which tables of ternary and diurnal logarithms will be required as given in *Sidereal Calculation Tables* by Mary Austin. We calculate thus:

| Longitude of the Sun | 14 37 17 | Libra |
|---|---|---|
| Long. Sun noon Oct. 8, 1959 | 14 27 28 | Libra |
| Subtract | 00 09 49 |  |
| Sun's motion Oct. 8/9 | 59 15 |  |

| | |
|---|---|
| Ternary log of difference | 1.26331 |
| Ternary log of Sun's motion | .48258 |
| Subtract | .78073 |

Look up this figure in the diurnal log tables. The antilogarithm will be found to be between 3h 58m and 3h 59m. Interpolation for complete accuracy will give 3h 58m 35s. Such accuracy is not always essential, especially when the natal time of birth is not known with precision.

We will calculate this map (Map E).

| | H M S |
|---|---|
| Astronomical time of solar return | 03 58 35 |
| Acceleration | 39 |
| S.T. Oct. 8, 1959 | 13 05 29 |
| S.T. Greenwich | 17 04 43 |
| Residence West of Greenwich | 39 |
| S.T. of S.S.R. | 17 04 04 |

The procedure for this calculation is simplified when a sidereal ephemeris is available. There is no sidereal ephemeris for 1959 but in order to exemplify the procedure we will convert the tropical noon longitude by the addition of the S.V.P.

| | | |
|---|---|---|
| Tropical long. of Sun noon Oct 8 | 14 27 28 | Libra |
| Synetic vernal point, Oct. 8 | 05 49 17 | |
| Add | 20 16 45 | Virgo |

Working from this figure:

| | | |
|---|---|---|
| Natal sidereal Sun | 20 26 34 | Virgo |
| Sidereal Sun noon Oct. 8 | 20 16 45 | |
| Subtract | 09 49 | |

which is the figure we previously obtained.

If a sidereal ephemeris is available, the noon longitude of the Sun is taken straight from it without any consideration of precession. In the sidereal zodiac there is no precession. The S.S.R. may be considered as a cyclic chart showing by its prominent formations the trend of the year. The principles of the interpretation of solar returns are given in Chapter XVIII as they differ considerably from ordinary tropical methods.

In Map E we would pay attention to the planets near an angle, i.e., Pluto, Venus and Uranus and to the Sun-Mars conjunction. We note too that solar Pluto is near conjunction with the

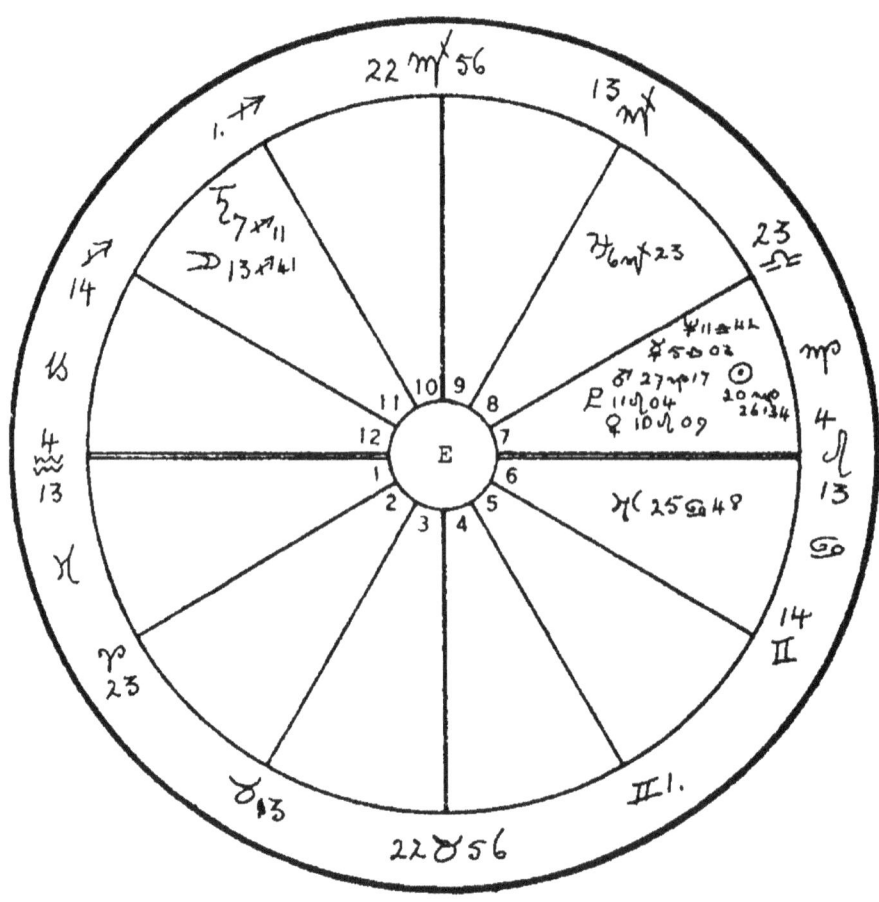

*Map E*
*Susan Walker, Sidereal Solar Return 1959*

natal Ascendant. We consider midpoints important and students will notice that the midpoint of Pluto and Uranus is near the Descendant. At times during the year all these formations, as well as the other planets, will become activated by progression and regression.

Although the S.S.R. is valid and undoubtedly progresses well during the whole year, it is often interesting to supplement it by drawing the Demisolar, calculated by the same method, for the time when the sidereal Sun reaches its opposition point.

# Chapter X

# The Solar Quotidian Progression

There are two methods of progressing a solar return or ingress, the Quotidian Method (explained in this chapter) and the Progressed Sidereal Solar Return (P.S.S.R) to be explained in Chapter XII. Although the rate of progression of the angles is different, experience shows that they are both valid. Calculated to a given date they may show different symbolism, but this is significant for the event. When this does occur the event is likely to be of greater importance, the different rates of progression showing different phases of the event. There are many factors which can enter into the manifestation of one event.

The Solar Quotidian (S.Q.) method is dependent on the increase of the right ascension of the mean Sun (M.S.) between the date of the return or ingress and the date and time of the event. The method of calculating the M.S. is given in Chapter IV. The rule for the calculation of the Solar Quotidians is to add the difference in M.S. to the S.T. of the return or ingress. The sum is the S.T. of the S.Q. No *bija* correction is required nor is there any necessity for the Equation of Time. An example will make the method clear.

Required: The Solar Quotidian for the S.S.R 1959 of Susan Walker, to March 27, 1960, 12 noon G.M.T., the day and time of the riding accident.

|  | H M S |
|---|---|
| Mean Sun (M.S.) noon, March 27, 1960 | 00 19 40 |
| M.S. of the S.S.R. 1959 | 13 06 08 |
| Difference | 11 13 32 |
| RAM.C. of S.S.R. 1959 (London) | 17 04 04 |
| Add RA.M.C. of the S.Q. | 04 17 36 |

The S.S.R. was calculated for London, the place of residence at the time. The accident occurred at Blewbury, Berkshire, which is at longitude 1W17 and latitude 51N30. This S.Q. has been calculated for the place of the S.S.R. and not for the place of the event. Opinion differs on this question but our present opinion is that the S.Q. and all progressions should be calculated for the place of the S.S.R. and not transposed to the place of the event. Here the difference in time (five minutes) is not great, but naturally it can make a considerable difference. The question is under investigation.

### Solar Quotidian Increments

| Days | H | M | S | Days | H | M | S |
|---|---|---|---|---|---|---|---|
| 1 | 0 | 3 | 56.6 | 10 | 0 | 39 | 25.6 |
| 2 | 0 | 7 | 53.1 | 20 | 1 | 18 | 51.1 |
| 3 | 0 | 11 | 49.7 | 30 | 1 | 58 | 16.7 |
| 4 | 0 | 15 | 46.2 | 40 | 2 | 37 | 42.2 |
| 5 | 0 | 19 | 42.8 | 50 | 3 | 17 | 07.8 |
| 6 | 0 | 23 | 39.3 | 60 | 3 | 56 | 33.4 |
| 7 | 0 | 27 | 35.9 | 70 | 4 | 35 | 58.9 |
| 8 | 0 | 31 | 32.4 | 80 | 5 | 15 | 24.5 |
| 9 | 0 | 35 | 29.0 | 90 | 5 | 54 | 50.0 |
| 10 | 0 | 39 | 25.6 | 100 | 6 | 34 | 15.6 |

| Days | H | M | S |
|---|---|---|---|
| 100 | 06 | 34 | 15.6 |
| 200 | 13 | 08 | 31.2 |
| 300 | 19 | 42 | 46.8 |

| Hours | M | S | Hours | M | S | Minutes | S |
|---|---|---|---|---|---|---|---|
| 1 | 0 | 09.9 | 13 | 2 | 08.1 | | |
| 2 | 0 | 19.7 | 14 | 2 | 18.0 | 4 | 1 |
| 3 | 0 | 29.6 | 15 | 2 | 27.9 | 10 | 2 |
| 4 | 0 | 39.4 | 16 | 2 | 37.7 | 16 | 3 |
| 5 | 0 | 49.3 | 17 | 2 | 47.6 | 22 | 4 |
| 6 | 0 | 59.1 | 18 | 2 | 57.4 | 28 | 5 |
| 7 | 1 | 09.0 | 19 | 3 | 07.3 | 34 | 6 |
| 8 | 1 | 18.9 | 20 | 3 | 17.1 | 40 | 7 |
| 9 | 1 | 28.7 | 21 | 3 | 27.0 | 46 | 8 |
| 10 | 1 | 38.6 | 22 | 3 | 36.8 | 52 | 9 |
| 11 | 1 | 48.4 | 23 | 3 | 46.7 | 58 | 10 |
| 12 | 1 | 58.3 | 24 | 3 | 56.6 | | |

The positions of the progressed quotidian planets should now be calculated for the progressed time of the map. This time is calculated as follows:

|                                      | H  M  S    |
|--------------------------------------|------------|
| Difference of M.S                    | 11 13 32   |
| Acceleration, minus                  | 01 50      |
|                                      | 11 11 42   |
| Add astronomical time (A.T.) S.S.R.  | 03 58 35   |
| A. T. of Solar Quotidian             | 15 10 07   |

We use A.T. as we are using a noon ephemeris. If we are using a midnight ephemeris we shall naturally be calculating in U.T. We therefore calculate the quotidian planets for 15h 10m 7s on Oct. 8, 1959, the day of the solar return. Only the Moon will show any major change from its solar position. Strictly we should show both solar and progressed positions as it has been found that, particularly with the Moon, both are valid.

The Solar Quotidian is shown in Map F. As the Earth's rotation on its axis is deemed to be perfectly constant when read in ephemeris time, a table can be prepared and used with accuracy for any number of days and hours following the date of the solar return. We give this table and will calculate the same S.Q. from it. We use the astronomical calendar (Chapter V).

| Day of event and time, A.T. | 393d 00h      | (366, leap year + 27) |
|-----------------------------|---------------|-----------------------|
| Day of S.S.R. and time, A.T. | 222d 03h 52m |                       |
| Subtract                    | 170d 20h 01m  |                       |

From the S.Q. table:

|            | H  M  S    |
|------------|------------|
| 100 days   | 06 34 15.6 |
| 70 days    | 04 35 58.9 |
| 20 hours   | 03 17.1    |
| 1 minute   |            |
| Add        | 11 13 32   |

which agrees precisely with our previous calculation.

In order to compute a series of quotidians for any given period or throughout the year, choose a starting point and for it calculate the S.T. of the S.Q. For an interval of seven days add successively 27m 35.9s, and for 10 days add 39m 25.6s. Those who like logarithms or have a calculator will find that the daily increase in hours is 0.06571, the logarithm of which is 8.81763 (-1.18237). These figures can be used for the rapid calculation of the increment of S.T. for any number of days.

Looking at Map F we note that natal Saturn and the natal progressed Ascendant are close to the S.Q. Ascendant and opposed to transiting Venus and Mercury. It was a Venus (pleasure) Mercury (ride) but it ran into natal Saturn on the Ascendant, a serious formation having con-

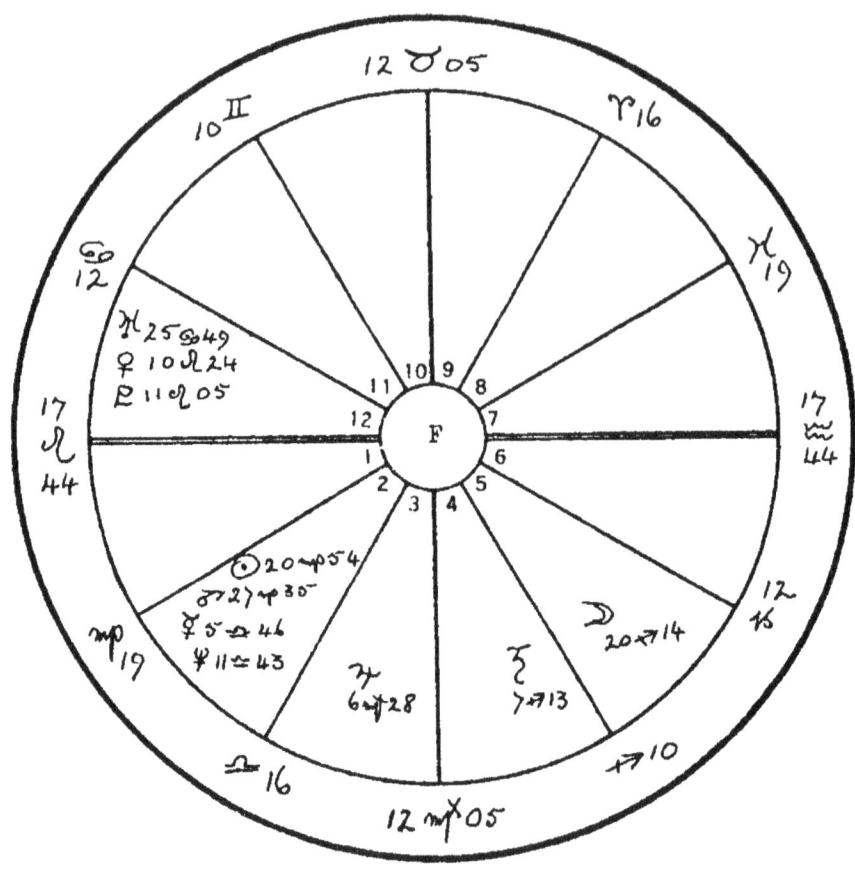

*Map F*
***Susan Walker, Solar Quotidian to March 27, 1960***

nection *inter alia* with falls. Natal planets often show where the native suffers the effect of the planet concerned.

## Chapter XI

# Progresson of Solar Planets

It should be possible to progress any valid map by any accepted method of progression. This could be a test for any of the many different methods of progressions which have been proposed in recent years.

The Arabic system of progression, day-to-year, or secondary method, has proved its worth. It has recently been discovered that planets in the solar return or ingress (known as solar planets) can be progressed by the secondary rate with very accurate results. On this basis it will be rare that solar planets, other than the Moon with an average motion of some 13 degrees a day-year, will close to an exact aspect during the year. It does happen with other planets, and it is this which, giving particular significance to that aspect, seems to give an important colouration to the events of the year.

Experience has shown that the progression of the Moon to the conjunction or opposition of any planet during the solar year gives a very accurate timing for an event of the nature of a planet. Generally this is true of those aspects between any two planets, but the timing will be less accurate as they remain within orbs for a longer time.

Experience shows that the only valid aspects for the progression of the planets of the solar return, known as solar planets, are the conjunction and opposition; zodiacal trines, sextiles and even squares do not produce noticeable events. This fact may appear peculiar to some astrologers, but it generally confirms experience in connection with the interpretation of solar returns. The important configurations are mundane and not zodiacal. It is possible that the closing of mundane squares will be effective but these are more difficult to calculate. This insistence on conjunctions and oppositions does cut down the number of solar returns in which these appear, but when they are present they are extremely valuable.

A study of these progressions throws light on the question of the interpretation of solar returns and ingresses. It seems clear that the really powerful aspects are those which become partile within 24 hours. These are the essential and active ingredients of the retuns. Other aspects may have little importance in themselves, but if coming simultaneously to angles, they attain the dignity of a mundane square, then it is different.

Examples will best show how these directions are calculated. Use will be made of the M.S., the calculation of which is explained in Chapter IV. It seems probable that the aspect to be considered is that between the progressed planet and a radical solar planet. The alternative is an aspect between both planets progressed. The difference in date of maturation is only slight, but the aspects to the radical seem to give more accurate results. It is probable that the whole period between the maturation of the radical and the progressed will be tinged by the planet concerned, and this may well have concrete effects. As the calculation is slightly different, we shall give examples of both types of aspect.

Example 1: In the Capricorn solar ingress for 1918, the Moon is applying to the conjunction of Venus. What is the date of maturation of this aspect? Let us find out. First we will calculate the time of the conjunction with the solar planet, Venus.

| | | |
|---|---|---|
| Radical Solar Venus | Aquarius 27 50 | (Tropical) |
| Moon noon Jan. 14 | Aquarius 14 41 51 | |
| Difference | 13 08 09 | log 0.26175 |
| Moon's motion, Jan. 14 | 14 45 02 | log 0.21141 |
| | | 0.05034 |

The antilogarithm of this figure is 21h 22m 36s, which is the A.T. of the conjunction.

| | H M S |
|---|---|
| A.T. of conj. of prog. Moon and solar Venus | 21 22 36 |
| A.T. of Sidereal Solar Ingress, 1918 | 01 35 24 |
| Difference | 19 47 12 |
| Acceleration | 03 15 |
| M.S. of date of ingress | 19 32 50 |
| M.S. of conjunction | 15 23 17 |

A glance at the 1918 ephemeris will show that the sidereal time at noon, which is also the noon M.S., on November 12 was 15h 23m 13s. Our Moon-Venus conjunction, a highly appropriate aspect, falls therefore one day later than the Armistice of November 11, 1918.

We shall now calculate the same conjunction of the Moon to the progressed Venus. This calculation is even simpler because the time of the conjunction is given in the ephemeris as 9:41 a.m., January 15.

|                      | H  M  S    |
|----------------------|------------|
| U.T. of conjunction  | 09 41      |
| U. T. of ingress     | 13 35      |
| Difference           | 20 06      |
| Acceleration         | 03 21      |
| M.S. of ingress      | 19 32 50   |
| M.S. of maturation   | 15 42 11   |

From the ephemeris it will be seen that this corresponds with November 17, six days after the Armistice.

Example 2: In the solar return of President Kennedy for 1962 the Moon is applying to the conjunction of Mars. When will this aspect mature? We shall use a sidereal ephemeris.

| Solar Mars           | Aries | 06 49 |                        |
|----------------------|-------|-------|------------------------|
| Solar Moon 12h D.T.  | Aries | 03 49 |                        |
| Difference           |       | 03 00 |                        |
|                      |       |       | 6 hour log 0.3010      |
| Moon's 6-hour motion |       | 03 36 | 6 hour log 0.2219      |
|                      |       |       | 0.0791                 |
|                      |       |       | (see Chapter XIV)      |

The antilogarithm of 0.0791 is 5h 00m which, added to 12h U.T., for which time we have taken the Moon, gives 1700 U.T. as the time of the conjunction of Moon and Mars.

|                                               | H  M  S   |
|-----------------------------------------------|-----------|
| U.T. of conj. of Moon prog. and radical Mars  | 17 00 00  |
| U.T. of S.S.R. 1962                           | 08 49 03  |
| Difference                                    | 08 10 57  |
| Acceleration                                  | 01 21     |
| M.S, of S.S.R. 1962                           | 04 29 33  |
| M.S. of date of maturation                    | 12 41 51  |
| M.S. of Oct. 3, 1962 at 0h U.T.               | 12 40 56  |
| Diff. equivalent to 5h 30m or 5:30 a.m. G.M.T.|       55  |

This corresponds to 11:30 p.m. October 1, at Oxford, Mississippi, the date campus riots took place resulting in the death of two people. The president had indeed taken vigorous action.

The first edition of this book, written in April 1961, stated, with reference to this aspect:

> "The ordinary man under this configuration may become a target for criticism to which he will react strongly even to

> the point of losing his temper. In the map of a national leader the aspect may well work in the mundane sphere and cause a vigorous reaction. Here could be a dangerous period."

It is interesting to note that the president's S.S.R. for 1962, when equated to Oxford, has Mars and therefore this conjunction with the Moon on the Ascendant. This is evidence that personal maps may be equated effectively to centres of interest. Moon progressed conjunction Mars progressed matures on October 9, 1962. A further example will help to illustrate our point.

Example 3: In Cyril Fagan's S.S.R. for 1948 the Moon was applying to the opposition of Uranus. What was the date of maturation of this opposition? In a 1948 ephemeris, the time of this opposition is given as May 24, the time being 7:30 p.m. G.M.T.

|  | H M S |
|---|---|
| U.T. of opposition | 19 30 00 |
| U.T. of S.S.R. | 20 18 53 |
| Difference | 23 11 07 |
| Acceleration | 03 49 |
| M.S. of S.S.R. | 04 05 29 |
| M.S. of date of maturation | 03 20 25 |

If we study the ephemeris for the following year and look in the column headed "Sidereal Time," we find this M.S. tallies with May 12, 1949, which is the date of maturation of Moon opposite Uranus. It was two days later, on May 14, 1949, that Cyril Fagan solved the problem of the *hypsomata* (exaltation degrees of the planets), reference to which has been made in Chapter II. Mercury also is in close conjunction with Uranus and enhances the eminent suitability of this formation as an important astrological discovery.

These progression of the solar Moon constitute an ideal method for rectification, even when the time of birth is unknown. A glance at the ephemeris at the time of the yearly S.S.R.s will show when the Moon is applying to the conjunction of, or opposition to, a planet. During the year there will be an event of the nature of the planet. If we know the date of an actual event, we can calculate the time of birth that will bring the Moon exactly to the conjunction of, or opposition to, the planet on the correct date.

An example will show how this rectification is made. Let us suppose that there was a violent loss of temper at 10 p.m. G.M.T. on August 17, 1960. The calculation is as follows:

|   |   |
|---|---|
|   | *H M S* |
| (a) *Bija* equivalent 10:00 p.m. G.M.T. | 00 01 38 |
| (b) S.T. Moon G.M.T., Aug. 17, 1960 | 09 43 28 |
| (c) M.S. of date and time of temper | 09 45 06 |
| (d) M.S. S.S.R. date, April 21, 1960 | 01 58 14 |
| (e) Difference | 07 46 52 |
| (f) Deduct *bija* equivalent 7h 47m | 01 17 |
| (g) Call this "Z" | 07 45 35 |
| (h) Time of conjunction Moon-Mars | 11 15 |
| (i) Required G.M.T. of S.S.R. (h) -(g) | 03 29 25 |

The S.S.R. therefore took place at 3:29:25 p.m. G.M.T. on April 21, 1960, at which time it will be found that the Sun's tropical longitude was at Taurus 1° 31′ 13″. If we deduct from this figure the accrued value of precession which is 42′ 06″, we arrive at the Sun's tropical longitude at birth, or Taurus 0° 49′ 07″, from which measurement the time of birth can easily be calculated. In order to check this, the calculation should be repeated on another suitable occasion and, possibly, with other configurations of planets. The types of events signified by the Moon with the planets will be:

| | |
|---|---|
| Moon-Pluto | Disruptive |
| Moon-Neptune | Mortifying or humiliating |
| Moon-Uranus | Thrill or shock |
| Moon-Saturn | Frustration, annoyance, inhibition |
| Moon-Jupiter | Expansion of feelings, success |
| Moon-Mars | Anger, energetic action |
| Moon-Venus | Pleasure, joy, ease, problems of relationship |
| Moon-Sun | Sexual stimulation, union or marriage, vigorous action |

It has recently been rediscovered that the Moon is the significator of carnal love. This fact in itself may help with the rectification of the birth time, when, for example, in the year of marriage the progressed solar Moon comes to the conjunction of, or opposition to, the Sun.

Apart from these solar progressions it will be found that on the dates the solar Moon or its progressed position comes to an angle the erotic appetites tend to become stimulated. When the progressed solar Moon conjoins or opposes the Sun, the effects are more pronounced and endure longer. Marriages and the like will usually find the solar Moon or its progressed position precisely on one of the angles of the P.S.S.R. or S.Q., usually the former.

As a confirmation of the above statements, the reader is referred to Carl Jung's statistical analysis for marriage in which he found that Sun-Moon contacts were highly significant for marriage, more so than Venus or Mars aspects.

These progressed lunars are most instructive and lead to the following conclusions:

(a) Zodiacal configurations must be taken geocentrically, i.e., without regard to parallax;

(b) Mutual configurations in right ascension appear to have no astrological influence;

(c) Only zodiacal conjunctions and oppositions appear to be effective;

(d) The Arabic or secondary system of directions is fully vindicated. Progressing the solar Moon by its radix or mean motion or by the one-degree method yields totally wrong dates of maturation.

# Chapter XII

# The Progressed Sidereal Solar Return (P.S.S.R.)

The solar return, by its prominent formations and by angular planets, will show the main trends of the year. Often the lunar returns will give an indication of the probable month for manifestations. Progressions of the solar return have been found to indicate closely the actual day of the event. This is an ideal which is frequently attained in practice but naturally requires an accurately rectified natus. If, however, it is found that events indicated by the progressions consistently fall a few days early or late, these progressions form a most valuable means of rectification of the birth map, the time of which can be adjusted so that aspects indicating events do fall on the correct day. We would assess the orb of the contact with the angles at some three days.

We have already discussed in Chapter X one method or progression, the solar Quotidian. We shall now deal with the other main method of progression, the Progressed Sidereal Solar Return, or P.S.S.R., for short. Both these methods of progression are valid and will not normally be found in contradiction. When, as often happens, they are in general agreement, it is more probable that an event of importance is maturing. Further study may show a basic difference between the interpretation of these two methods. Meanwhile they can both be used with confidence.

The principle behind the rate of progression in this method of the sidereal time and therefore of the angles of the solar return lies in calculating the difference in the sidereal time of two consecutive solar returns, adding 24 hours and dividing the sum by the mean length of the sidereal year, 365.253842 days. The result will give the daily increase in sidereal time to be added to that of the solar return.

## Increase of Sidereal Time

| Days | H | M | S | Days | H | M | S |
|---|---|---|---|---|---|---|---|
| 1 | 0 | 04 | 57 | 20 | 1 | 39 | 08 |
| 2 | 0 | 09 | 55 | 30 | 2 | 28 | 42 |
| 3 | 0 | 14 | 52 | 40 | 3 | 18 | 16 |
| 4 | 0 | 19 | 50 | 50 | 4 | 07 | 50 |
| 5 | 0 | 24 | 47 | 60 | 4 | 57 | 24 |
| 6 | 0 | 29 | 44 | 70 | 5 | 46 | 58 |
| 7 | 0 | 34 | 42 | 80 | 6 | 36 | 32 |
| 8 | 0 | 39 | 39 | 90 | 7 | 26 | 06 |
| 9 | 0 | 44 | 37 | 100 | 8 | 15 | 40 |
| 10 | 0 | 49 | 34 | 200 | 16 | 31 | 21 |
|  |  |  |  | 300 | 0 | 47 | 01 |

## The Equation of Time Table

| Jan | 1 | − 3 | Mar | 28 | − 5 | Aug | 10 | − 5 | Oct | 19 | + 15 |
|---|---|---|---|---|---|---|---|---|---|---|---|
|  | 2 | − 4 | Apr | 1 | − 4 |  | 16 | − 4 |  | 24 | + 16 |
|  | 4 | − 5 |  | 4 | − 3 |  | 21 | − 3 | Nov | 15 | + 15 |
|  | 6 | − 6 |  | 7 | − 2 |  | 25 | − 2 |  | 20 | + 14 |
|  | 8 | − 7 |  | 11 | − 1 |  | 29 | − 1 |  | 24 | + 13 |
|  | 11 | − 8 |  | 15 | 0 | Sep | 1 | 0 |  | 28 | + 12 |
|  | 13 | − 9 |  | 19 | + 1 |  | 4 | + 1 | Dec | 1 | + 11 |
|  | 16 | − 0 |  | 23 | + 2 |  | 8 | + 2 |  | 4 | + 10 |
|  | 19 | − 1 |  | 29 | + 3 |  | 10 | + 3 |  | 6 | + 9 |
|  | 23 | − 12 | May | 9 | + 4 |  | 13 | + 4 |  | 8 | + 8 |
|  | 27 | − 13 |  | 23 | + 3 |  | 15 | + 5 |  | 11 | + 7 |
| Feb | 2 | − 14 | Jun | 1 | + 2 |  | 18 | + 6 |  | 13 | + 6 |
|  | 24 | − 13 |  | 7 | + 1 |  | 22 | + 7 |  | 15 | + 5 |
| Mar | 2 | − 12 |  | 13 | 0 |  | 24 | + 8 |  | 17 | + 4 |
|  | 7 | − 11 |  | 17 | − 1 |  | 27 | + 9 |  | 19 | + 3 |
|  | 11 | − 10 |  | 22 | − 2 |  | 30 | + 10 |  | 21 | + 2 |
|  | 14 | − 9 |  | 27 | − 3 | Oct | 3 | + 11 |  | 23 | + 1 |
|  | 18 | − 8 | Jul | 1 | − 4 |  | 6 | + 12 |  | 25 | − 0 |
|  | 22 | − 7 |  | 7 | − 5 |  | 9 | + 13 |  | 27 | − 1 |
|  | 25 | − 6 |  | 14 | − 6 |  | 14 | + 14 |  | 29 | − 2 |
|  |  |  |  |  |  |  |  |  |  | 31 | − 3 |

This means that for accurate work we must calculate the S.T. of the current solar return and also that for the following year. We shall give later details of such a precision method. Often sufficient accuracy can be obtained by the use of the following table which is based on the average difference between two consecutive solar returns, 30 hours 9 minutes and 13 seconds. The sidereal time of a return thus progresses during the year and finally gives the time of the next solar return. Thus, there is a continuous progression of the angles of the return from birth to death at an approximate rate of 5 minutes a day.

The use of this table will be made clear by an example. We will calculate the approximate S.T. of our example horoscope to the date of the accident, March 27, 1960. The period elapsed since the S.S.R. 1959 is 171 days and 8 hours.

From the table:

|  | H | M | S |
|---|---|---|---|
| 100 days | 08 | 15 | 40 |
| 70 days | 05 | 46 | 58 |
| 20 hours |  | 04 | 07 |
|  | 04 | 06 | 45 |
| Add S.T. of the S.S.R. | 17 | 04 | 04 |
| Uncorrected S.T. P.S.S.R. | 07 | 10 | 49 |

This figure is approximate only as we have to allow for the difference between apparent or sun dial time and mean time. To do this the S.T. must be corrected by the equation of time. We use the table for the equation of time.

Date of S.S.R. Oct. 8        Equation of time plus 13 minutes
Date of event, March 27     Equation of time minus 5 minutes

Change the sign of the lower line and add.

Thus       plus 13
             plus  5
             plus 18

We therefore add 18 minutes to the S.T. already found, making the R.A.M.C. of the P.S.S.R 7h 29m to the nearest minute. We will anticipate our precise calculation by saying that this gives 7h 36m, a difference of 7 minutes S.T. It can be more than this. This method can, however, be recommended for rapid calculation particularly when the birth time is uncertain.

It will be noted that the P.S.S.R. has been drawn for the place of residence at the time of the S.S.R. It is open to question whether the P.S.S.R. should not be drawn for the place of the event. We advise experiment on this point. For the moment the student would be well advised to draw for the place of the S.S.R.

For those who enjoy logarithms or have a calculator there is another method. The daily difference in S.T. for the average difference between consecutive solar returns must first be calculated. This is:

**Average Difference Between Returns**
True Length of the Sidereal Year

In figures this is

$$\frac{30h\ 09m\ 13s}{365.253842} \quad \text{or} \quad \frac{108553\ \text{seconds}}{365.253842}$$

This equation can be solved by logarithms or a calculator. The daily increase of S.T. is 4m 57.197s. In practice it is often more useful to express this in decimals of an hour or, .082555 hours per day.

Those who would calculate their progressions throughout the year will find this method useful. At intervals of a week the average advance is .577885 hours (34m 40s) or for ten days the figure is .82555 hours (49m 32s). The addition or subtraction of the Equation of Time must not be forgotten.

**The Precision Method**

We will now calculate for the same event using the precision method invented by Garth Allen and further developed by Alexander Marr who has produced special logarithms which we reproduce with his kind permission. See table.

The date of the event is March 27, 1960, at noon G.M.T. As use is made of the right ascension of the Sun, we will explain how this can be calculated as it is generally not given in the ephemeris. It is, however, given in Stahl's sidereal ephemerides. We use any tropical table of houses and consider the tropical longitude of the Sun as the cusp of the tenth house (M.C.). The corresponding S.T. will be the right ascension of the Sun. For example, if the tropical Sun is in 6 Aries, we see that 6 Aries in the M.C. column is equivalent to a sidereal time of 0h 22m 02s which is accordingly the required R.A. For minutes of the Sun's longitude we must interpolate.

To find log Y we must calculate the sidereal time of the year following the event, 1960.

|  | H M S |
|---|---|
| S.T.S.S.R. 1960 | 23 20 22 |
| S.T.S.S.R. 1959 | 17 04 04 |
| Subtract | 06 16 18 (Add 24 hours to get 30h 16m 18s for next calculation.) |

## P.S.S.R. AND RSSR TABLES (LOG Y)

| *29 hours* | | | *30 hours* | | | *30 hours* | | | *30 hours* | | |
|---|---|---|---|---|---|---|---|---|---|---|---|
| 53m | 00s | 0.09520 | 00m | 00s | 0.09689 | 07m | 00s | 0.09857 | 14m | 00s | 0.10025 |
|  | 15 | 526 |  | 15 | 695 |  | 15 | 863 |  | 15 | 031 |
|  | 30 | 532 |  | 30 | 701 |  | 30 | 869 |  | 30 | 037 |
|  | 45 | 538 |  | 45 | 717 |  | 45 | 875 |  | 45 | 043 |
| 54m | 00s | 544 | 01m | 00s | 713 | 08m | 00s | 881 | 5m | 00s | 049 |
|  | 15 | 550 |  | 15 | 719 |  | 15 | 887 |  | 15 | 055 |
|  | 30 | 556 |  | 30 | 725 |  | 30 | 893 |  | 30 | 061 |
|  | 45 | 562 |  | 45 | 731 |  | 45 | 899 |  | 45 | 067 |
| 55m | 00s | 568 | 02m | 00s | 737 | 09m | 00s | 905 | 16m | 00s | 173 |
|  | 15 | 574 |  | 15 | 743 |  | 15 | 911 |  | 15 | 179 |
|  | 30 | 580 |  | 30 | 749 |  | 30 | 917 |  | 30 | 085 |
|  | 45 | 586 |  | 45 | 755 |  | 45 | 923 |  | 45 | 091 |
| 56m | 00s | 592 | 03m | 00s | 761 | 10m | 00s | 929 | 17m | 00s | 097 |
|  | 15 | 598 |  | 15 | 767 |  | 15 | 935 |  | 15 | 0.10103 |
|  | 30 | 604 |  | 30 | 773 |  | 30 | 941 |  | 30 | 109 |
|  | 45 | 610 |  | 45 | 779 |  | 45 | 947 |  | 45 | 115 |
| 57m | 00s | 616 | 04m | 00s | 785 | 11m | 00s | 953 | 18m | 00s | 121 |
|  | 15 | 622 |  | 15 | 791 |  | 15 | 959 |  | 15 | 127 |
|  | 30 | 629 |  | 30 | 797 |  | 30 | 965 |  | 30 | 133 |
|  | 45 | 635 |  | 45 | 803 |  | 45 | 971 |  | 45 | 139 |
| 58m | 00s | 641 | 05m | 00s | 809 | 12m | 00s | 977 | 9m | 00s | 145 |
|  | 15 | 647 |  | 15 | 815 |  | 15 | 983 |  | 15 | 151 |
|  | 30 | 653 |  | 30 | 821 |  | 30 | 989 |  | 30 | 157 |
|  | 45 | 659 |  | 45 | 827 |  | 45 | 995 |  | 45 | 163 |
| 59m | 00s | 665 | 06m | 00s | 833 | 13m | 00s | 0.10001 | 20m | 00s | 169 |
|  | 15 | 671 |  | 15 | 839 |  | 15 | 007 |  | 15 | 169 |
|  | 30 | 677 |  | 30 | 845 |  | 30 | 013 |  | 30 | 181 |
|  | 45 | 683 |  | 45 | 851 |  | 45 | 019 |  | 45 | 187 |
|  | 60 | 689 |  | 60 | 857 |  | 60 | 025 |  | 60 | 193 |

Diff. Const. 6/15   1s +0   5s +2   9s +4   13s +5
                    2s +1   6s +2   10s +4  14s +6
                    3s +1   7s +3   11s +4
                    4s +2   8s +3   12s +5

(Compliments of Alexander Marr)

Adding 24 hours we see from the Log Y table that log Y for 1959/60 is .10080.

Our calculation is now as follows:

|  | H M S |  |
|---|---|---|
| RA. of Sun for event | 00 25 04 | Ternary log .19386 |
| R.A. of Sun S.S.R 1959 | 12 53 50 | Ternary log .10080 |
| [Ed. Note: Subtracting | 11 31 14] | 1.09306 |
| Subtract. Ternary antilog | 14 31 42* | |

* [Ed. Note: This result can be arrived at as follows: Divide 30h 16m 48s by 24 hours. Multiply the resultant by 11h 31m 14s. This gives 14h 31m 42s.]

Note that the ternary logarithm for the difference of right ascension is found from the ternary table in *Sidereal Calculation Tables* by treating hours as minutes and minutes as seconds, the seconds being found by

|  | H M S |
|---|---|
| S.T. increment to March 27, 1960 | 14 31 42 |
| S.T. S.S.R 1959 | 17 04 04 |
| S.T. P.S.S.R | 07 35 46 |

Map G has been drawn for the S.T. for London. The time for the calculation of the progressed planets is the same as that for the S.Q. (Chapter X). The progressed planets of the P.S.S.R. are the same as those of the S.Q. Other than the Moon they will only change slightly but the position of the progressed Moon is important. We see that the Sun and Mars bestride the Ascendant, the Sun being in exact conjunction with natal Neptune. Saturn transits near the I.C. and progressed Moon.

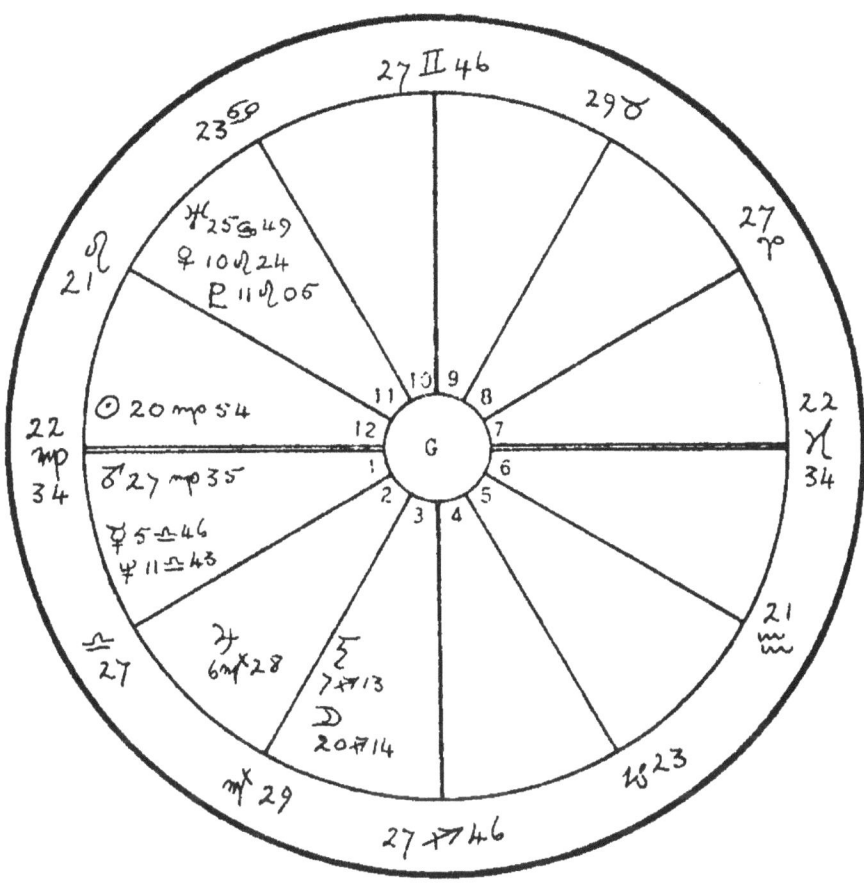

*Map G*
*Susan Walker, Progressed Sidereal Solar Return to March 27, 1960*

## Chapter XIII

# Regressions

Many astrologers consider that a horoscope as well as being progressed forwards in time can also be regressed backwards. If this is difficult to understand from a logical point of view, this difficulty may well lie in our failure to understand the true nature of time. A strong supporter of the theory of regressions is R.C. Davison, president of the Astrological Lodge of Great Britain, who has developed this theme at length in his book *The Technique of Prediction.*

Alexander Marr has been further developing this theory and has applied it to sidereal techniques, including regressions of the solar return by both rates and also by his use of converse solar and lunar returns. We gladly include in this book (with his kind pennission) some of his theories and recommend them to the attention of students. We ourselves have no doubt of the validity of these regressed return maps. Marr considers that it is illogical to insert in a regressed map only the actual transits of the day of the event. He also inserts the transits for that day which lies the same number of days before the solar return as the event lies after the solar. He has named these co-transits. To clarify this we will calculate the date for the co-transits for our example event on March 27, 1960.

|  | *Year* | *Day* | *H* | *M* |
|---|---|---|---|---|
| Event, March 27, 1960 U.T. | 1960 | 27 | 12 | 00 |
| S.S.R. Oct. 8, 1959 U.T. | 1959 | 222 | 15 | 59 |
| Difference in days and hours |  | 170 | 20 | 01 |
| Subtract from line above | 1959 | 51 | 19 | 58 |

This figure gives the date and time of the co-transits which are thus: April 29, 1959, 19h 58m U.T. Planets should be calculated for this date and time and inserted in the regressed returns as co-transits. Direct transits of the day of event are also valid and should be shown.

## The Solar Quotidian Regressed (S.Q.R.)

This quotidian is calculated in a similar manner to the direct S.Q. The only difference is that the difference between the M.S. of the event and that of the S.S.R. is subtracted and not added. We have already found in Chapter X that this difference is 11h 13m 32s. Our calculation is therefore:

|  | H M S |
|---|---|
| S.T. of S.S.R. 1969 | 17 04 04 |
| Difference of M.S. | 11 13 32 |
| S.T. of S.Q.R. | 05 50 32 |

The time used for the calculation of the regressed planets of the solar return is obtained as shown in Chapter X. In the S.Q.R. we shall deduct instead of adding. Thus:

|  | H M S |  |
|---|---|---|
| U.T. of S.S.R. | 15 58 35 | |
| Subtract | 11 13 32 | |
| U.T. of S.Q.R. | 04 45 03 | Oct. 8 |

See Map H. The value of the co-transit of Mars near the M.C. and in conjunction with natal Uranus is clearly shown. The Moon has regressed to a close conjunction with natal Saturn near the I.C. The transit of Jupiter, the preserver, near the I.C. may signify the skilled medical attention which saved Susan's life or simply Providence.

## The Regressed Sideral Solar Return (R.S.S.R.)

We shall now calculate the Regressed Sidereal Solar Return (R.S.S.R.) (using the P.S.S.R. rate) for March 27, 1960, the day of the accident. We shall first obtain our approximate figure by using the P.S.S.R. table as given in Chapter XII. For the difference of time of 170 days and 20 hours we obtain as before 14h 09m 14s. This figure must be subtracted (not added as with the P.S.S.R.) from the S.T. of the S.S.R. Thus:

|  | H M S |
|---|---|
| S.T. of S.S.R. | 17 04 04 |
| Subtract | 14 06 45 |
| Uncorrected S.T. | 02 57 19 |

As before, we have to correct for the Equation of Time, but here we must use the date we have found with the S.Q.R. for the co-transits, April 20, 1959, 19h 58m U,T, and not the date of the event.

From the Equation of Time Table in Chapter XII we find:

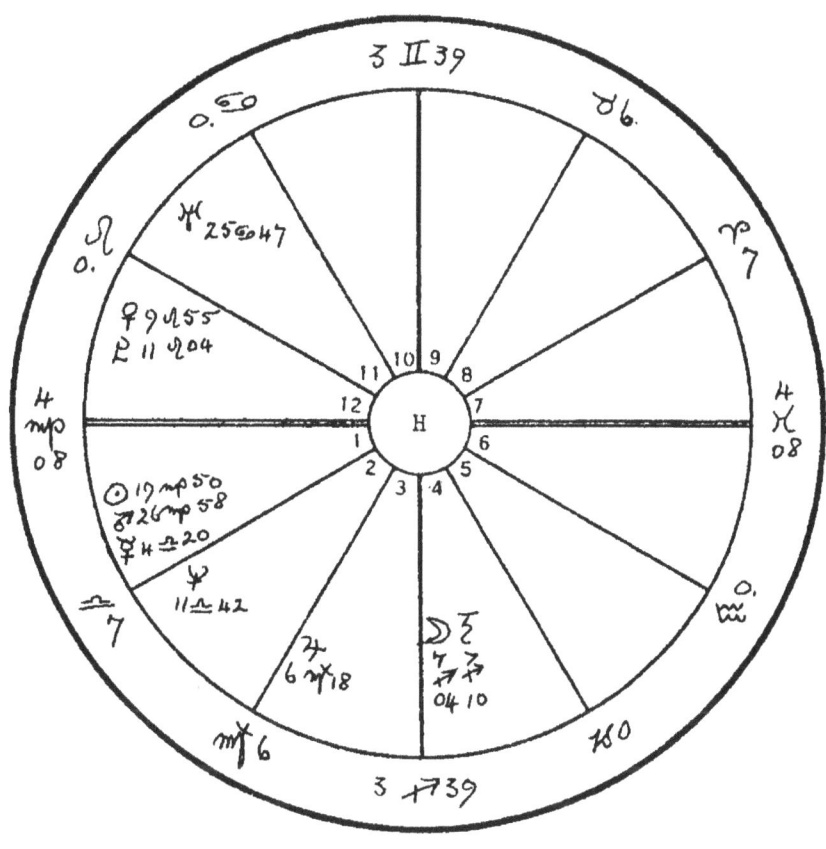

*Map H*
*Susan Walker, Solar Quotidian Regressed to March 27, 1960*

    Equation of Time, Oct. 1        plus 13
    Equation of Time, April 20     plus  1

Changing the sign of the lower line and adding we have plus 12, which we must add to the uncorrected S.T., making the S.T. of the R.S.S.R. 3h 09m 19s. This is our rapid method of obtaining an approximate answer.

As an additional example of the precise Garth Allen-Marr method we will calculate accurately this R.S.S.R. To do this we have to calculate the S.S.R. for 1958.

|  | H M S |
|---|---|
| S.T. of S.S.R. 1959 | 17 04 04 |
| S.T. of S.S.R. 1958 | 10 55 01 |
| Difference in S.T. | 06 09 03 |

From Marr's table, log Y for 1958/59 is 0.09906.

We have to calculate the right ascension of the Sun for the date and time of co-transits. To do this we use any tropical table of houses and consider the tropical Sun's longitude as the cusp of the tenth house (M.C.). The corresponding S.T. will be the right ascension of the Sun. Thus, if the tropical Sun is in 6 Aries, we see that 6 Aries in the M.C. column is equivalent to a sidereal time of 0h 22m 02s which is accordingly the required R.A. For minutes of the Sun's longitude we must interpolate. In Stahl's sidereal ephemerides, the R.A. of the Sun is given. Our calculation is therefore:

|  | H M S |
|---|---|
| R.A. Sun, co-transit day | 01 48 23 |
| RA. Sun S.S.R. 1959 | 12 53 50 |
| Difference | 11 05 27 |
|  |  |
| Ternary log difference | 1.21031 |
| log Y 1958/59 | .09906 |
| Subtract | 1.11125 |

The ternary antilogarithm of this figure is 13h 55m 57s which is the required decrease in sidereal time for the R.S.S.R.

|  | H M S |
|---|---|
| S.T. of S.S.R | 17 04 04 |
| Decrease of S.T. | 13 55 57 |
| S.T. of R.S.S.R. | 03 08 07 |

By our rapid method we had already found that the S.T. was approximately 3h 09m. In this case the difference is only about one minute but it can be much larger.

See Map I. The main significator of the event in this map is Uranus conjunct natal Mars exactly square the M.C. This zodiacal square to the M.C. is most important possibly because it is the midpoint between the M.C. and the I.C. Transiting Pluto in mundo rises with 3 Leo 30 near the Ascendant. The co-transit of Pluto is also near the Ascendant in 7 Leo 30. The "crisis" planet is thus strongly in evidence. If we consider natal planets, the midpoint of natal Mars and Saturn falls exactly in the same point.

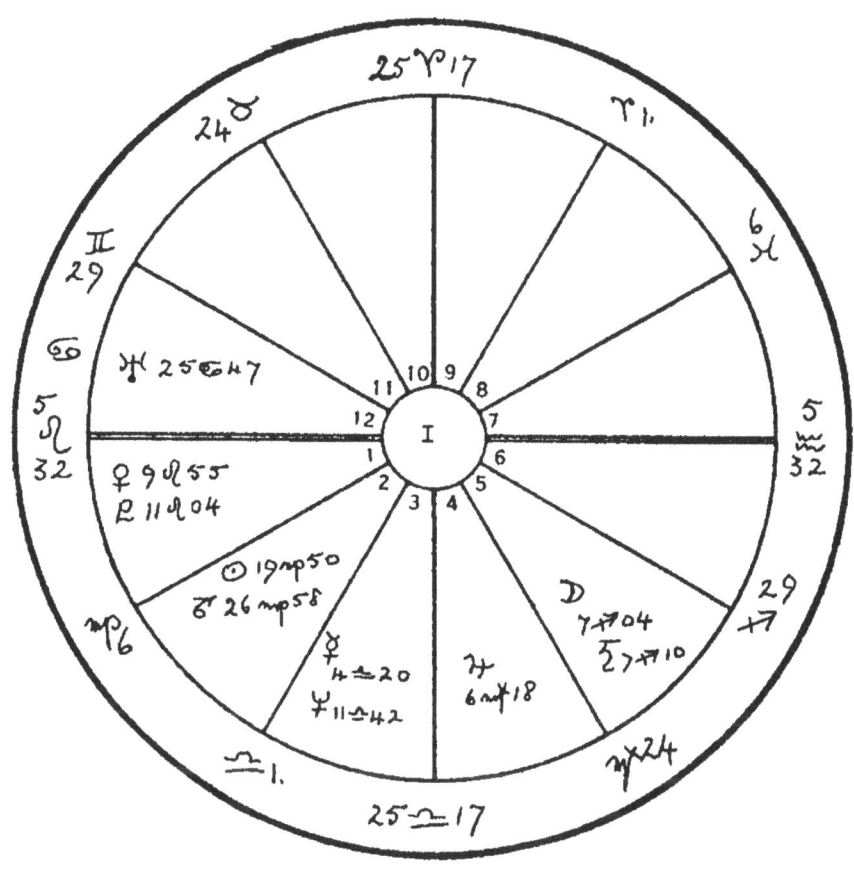

*Map I*
*Susan Walker, Regressed Sidereal Solar Return to March 27, 1960*

Chapter XIV

# The Sidereal Lunar Return

The Sidereal Lunar Return (S.L.R.) is a cyclic chart based on the return of the transiting Moon to its sidereal natal position. This chart thus relates directly to the natal map. We have to determine the day and time each month when the Moon returns to its natal position. Owing to the speed of the Moon, sufficient accuracy can be obtained by the use of diurnal logarithms.

We will first calculate a sidereal lunar return based on a natal Moon of our example horoscope, using a tropical Raphael ephemeris for 1960. The sidereal natal Moon is in 1 Aries 06. The Moon returns to this position on March 1, 1960, for the period covering the accident.

Our first step is to discover the equivalent value of this sidereal Moon in the tropical zodiac, taking into account the accrued precession. This we do by deducting the current value of the synetic vernal point from the sidereal position. Thus:

| | | |
|---|---|---|
| Natal Moon | 01 06 Aries | |
| S.V.P. March 1, 1960 | 05 49 | |
| Adding 30° to the top line the | | |
| Tropical Moon for this lunar is | 25 17 Aries | |
| | | |
| Tropical Moon | 25 17 Aries | |
| Moon, noon Feb. 29 | 13 54 Aries | |
| Difference | 11 23 | Diurnal log .32394 |
| Moon's motion Feb. 29 | 12 48 | Diurnal log .27300 |
| Diurnal antilog of this is 21h 21m | | .05094 |

We will calculate this map.

|  | H M S |
|---|---|
| Astronomical time | 21 21 |
| Acceleration | 03 30 |
| S.T. Noon Feb. 29 | 22 33 13 |
| S. T. Greenwich | 19 57 43 |
| Birthplace, West | 39 |
| S.T. Lunar Return | 19 57 04 |

These lunar returns should be cast for the place of residence on the date of the return, in this case Kensington, London. See Map J. Mars and Uranus, the latter conjunct natal Mars, which form an accident combination, are angular. Their midpoint in Aries 17 is opposite Neptune. A highly dangerous map.

Although it is probable that these lunar returns can be progressed we have not found any reliable method. It will be noted here that Mars and Uranus are wide of the angles. The event occurred at the extreme end of the lunar month which indicates the possibility of a progression and the fact that planets wide of the angles may tend to act later in the month. On the other hand planets very close to the angles may well act early after the date of the return.

Another method of using a tropical ephemeris is to transpose the tropical longitude at noon or midnight into the sidereal by the deduction of the S.V.P.

|  | D M |
|---|---|
| Here the noon tropical longitude is | 12 54 Aries |
| Add S.V.P. and go back one sign | 05 49 |
|  | 19 43 Pisces |
| Using this figure, |  |
| Sidereal Moon | 01 06 Aries |
| Sidereal noon position | 19 43 Pisces |
| Difference | 11 23 |

This is the same figure which we have already found.

From 1961, Stahl's sidereal ephemerides give the position of the Moon at 6-hour intervals in order to obtain greater accuracy. In order to take easy advantage of these 6-hour positions, a special table of 6-hour logarithms has been prepared by Alexander Marr and is reproduced here with his permission.

We will calculate a lunar return using this table.

Required S.L.R. for July 21, 1965, using Stahl's sidereal ephemeris.

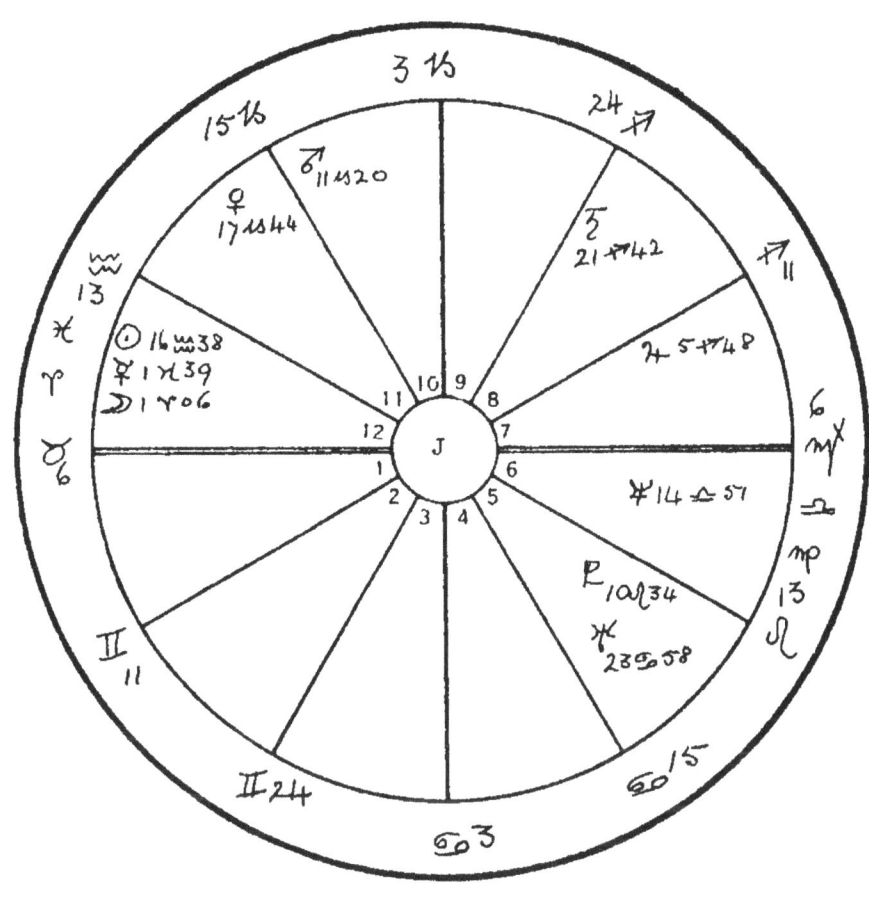

*Map J*
*Susan Walker, Sidereal Lunar Return*

| | | |
|---|---|---|
| Natal sidereal Moon | 01 06 | Aries |
| Moon 0600h U.T. July 21 | 28 06 | Pisces |
| Difference | 03 00 | 6h log .30103 |
| 6-hour motion | 03 13 | 6h log .27075 |
| Antilog 5h 36m | | .03028 |

To this figure we must not forget to add the 6 hours U.T. which was our starting point, making the U.T. of the return 11h 36m.

Although this lunar is the main lunar of the month and is valid for the entire period as our example shows, there is no doubt that the demilunar is of great importance especially when it throws up a figure with planets close to the angles, or with other important configurations. For this reason, they should not be neglected in a complete study. They are calculated for the return of the Moon to the opposition of its natal position.

# Chapter XV

# The Anlunar Return

The Anlunar Return is based on the monthly return of the Moon to its sidereal position in the annual solar return. The method of calculation is exactly the same as the for the lunar return but in order to give another example we will calculate it using a tropical ephemeris for 1960, the year of the event on March 27.

The sidereal solar Moon is 13 Sagittarius 41. As we are using a tropical ephemeris we must convert this to the tropical position by the addition of the accrued precession. The simplest way to do this is to deduct the current S.V.P. and go forward one sign. The current S.V.P. being 5°49′, the tropical position which we must use will be 7 Capricorn 52.

| | |
|---|---|
| Moon's tropical position | 07 52 Capricorn |
| Moon, noon, March 20, 1960 | 02 49 Capricorn |
| Difference | 05 03 Diurnal log .67692 |
| Moon's motion March 20/21 | 14 10 Diurnal log .22894 |
| Subtract. Antilog 8h 34m | .44798 |

Calculating:

| | H M S |
|---|---|
| Astronomical time | 08 34 |
| Acceleration | 01 24 |
| S.T. March 20 | 23 52 04 |
| S. T. Greenwich | 08 27 28 |
| Kensington, West | 39 |
| S. T. Anlunar | 08 26 49 |

Anlunars are drawn for the place of residence at the time of the return. See Map K. We note that the anlunar again presents the accident formation of an angular Uranus conjunct natal Mars and Pluto and opposite Mars. In addition it introduces a prominent Neptune (uncon-

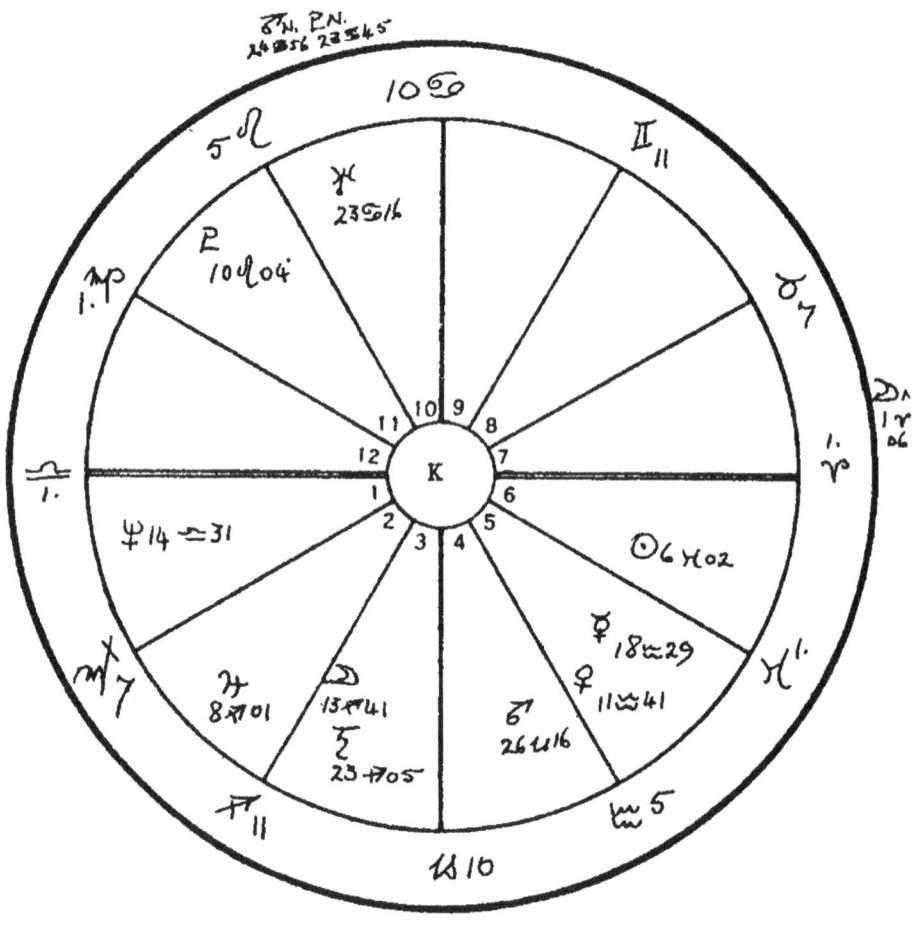

*Map K*
*Susan Walker, Anlunar Return*

sciousness) with the natal Moon exactly conjunct the Descendant. The demianlunar for the opposition of the Moon to its solar position may also be calculated and when appropriate will give additional information.

## Chapter XVI

# Kinetic Returns

We have already dealt with returns, solar and lunar, which are based on a static luminary, i.e. on the natal Sun or Moon or in the anlunar return on the Moon of the solar return. The returns which we are now considering have been christened "kinetic," moving or dynamic. Several possibilities present themselves: returns based on the progressed secondary Sun, the progressed solar return Moon or the progressed secondary Moon. Alexander Marr has made a special study of these kinetic returns and considers them of considerable value. A description of what was then called the lunar kinetic, which started the theory of kinetic returns, appeared in an early *SPICA* in an article by Cyril Fagan.

So we have no doubt that these kinetic returns are valid. The progressed position of any planet is a sensitive point on the basis of which a cyclic chart may be constructed. They may well prove to be of great importance. Possibly because they are more difficult to calculate they have not been fully tested. They may well prove to be of great importance. With further study we may detect a different basis for their inrerpretation. We hope that students will study these returns and assist in the forming of an opinion.

The authors of this book are fully aware of the problems raised by the introduction of further solar and lunar return methods. The standard solar and lunar returns are of proven value. They may help with the solution of a difficult problem in astrology, the determination of the scale of effect of an aspect or transit. We need to give judgment on its importance in the life of the native. We have found that, when astrological symbolism is repeated in different maps, the event indicated is more likely to be of vital importance. In this fact may lie the justification for using several methods involving progressions as well as regressions and of calculating kinetic as well as static return maps.

We will now study three kinetic returns, the solar kinetic, the solunar kinetic and the natal quotidian lunar kinetic.

## The Solar Kinetic

The Solar Kinetic Return (S.K.R.) is based on the return of the Sun to its secondary progressed longitude at the time of the ordinary solar return. It has been found that the angular planets in these returns often indicate with even greater clarity than the solar return the main trend of the year. We shall calculate the Solar Kinetic Return for our example horoscope. We must first find the day and time for the calculation of the progressed Sun. We proceed as follows:

Natus, 1949, Oct. 7    Day 221 14h 33m
Age 10, add                          10
                                    Day 231 14h 33m

Day 231 from the astronomical calendar (Chapter V) is Oct. 17, 1949. We must now calculate the exact position of the Sun for this day and time. We are using a tropical ephemeris, there being no sidereal ephemeris for this year.

Time 14h 33m              Diurnal log .21735
Sun's motion, Oct. 17/18  Ternary log .48003
Add                       Ternary log .69738

The ternary antilogarithm of this figure is 36m 08s. Adding this to the position of the Sun at noon, 23° 46′ 46″, we find that the progressed Sun in the tropical zodiac is 24° 22′ 54″. As we are working in the sidereal zodiac, we must add the accrued precession.

S.V.P. natus              05 57 45
S.V.P. Oct. 18, 1959      05 49 17
Accrued precession           08 28

Adding this figure to the position of the tropical Sun previously obtained we find that the tropical position of the Sun which we must use for working out our solar kinetic for 1959 is 24° 31′ 22″ Libra. If we are working with a sidereal ephemeris there is less difficulty because in the sidereal zodiac there is no precession.

We will now calculate the Solar Kinetic Return for 1959 in the same way as we calculate an ordinary solar return.

Progressed Sun               24 31 22 Libra (T.Z.)
Sun's motion, Oct. 18/19, 1959   24 21 25 Libra
Difference                   09 57 Ternary log 1.25745
Sun's motion, Oct. 18/19     59 35 Ternary log  .48015
Subtract                                        .77730

The diurnal antilogarithm of this figure is 4h 00m 28s which is the time of the Solar Kinetic. Calculating this kinetic:

|  | H M S |
|---|---|
| Time G.M.T. P.M. | 04 00 28 |
| Acceleration | 40 |
| S.T. Oct. 18, 1959 | 13 44 55 |
| S.T. Greenwich | 17 46 03 |
| Birthplace West | 39 |
| S.T. Solar Kinetic | 17 45 24 |

See Map L. The feature of this map is Saturn near the M.C., which is certainly suitable for the main event of the year. There was a Saturnian year to follow. Transiting Jupiter in conjunction with Saturn may have helped to ward off the worst effects. It is doubtful whether the Solar Kinetic can be progressed.

## The Solunar Kinetic

This kinetic return, formerly known as the lunar kinetic, has been renamed the solunar kinetic to show that it is based on the progressed Moon of the solar return. We shall calculate this return map for our example horoscope. Our first task is to find the day preceding the event on which the transiting Moon will be in the degree of the progressed solar return Moon. From Map E we see that the solar return Moon was in 13 Sagittarius 41. The accident occurred nearly six months after the date of the solar return. With the Moon moving at the rate of approximately one degree a month we see that it will be about 20 Sagittarius. This is its sidereal degree so that, if we are using a tropical ephemeris we must transpose it to the tropical making its degree about 14 Capricorn. The Moon transits over this longitude on March 20, 1960.

We must now calculate the exact progressed solar Moon. We will make use of the M.S. (Chapter IV). We will calculate for noon for convenience as we are using a noon ephemeris.

|  | H M S |
|---|---|
| M.S. March 20, 1960 | 23 56 01 |
| M.S. S.S.R. 1959 | 13 06 08 |
| Subtract | 10 49 53 |
| Subtract *bija* (Chapter VII) | 01 47 |
|  | 10 48 06 |
| Add A.T. of S.S.R. 1959 | 03 58 35 |
| A.T. for progressed Moon | 14 46 41 |

We will calculate this progressed Moon.

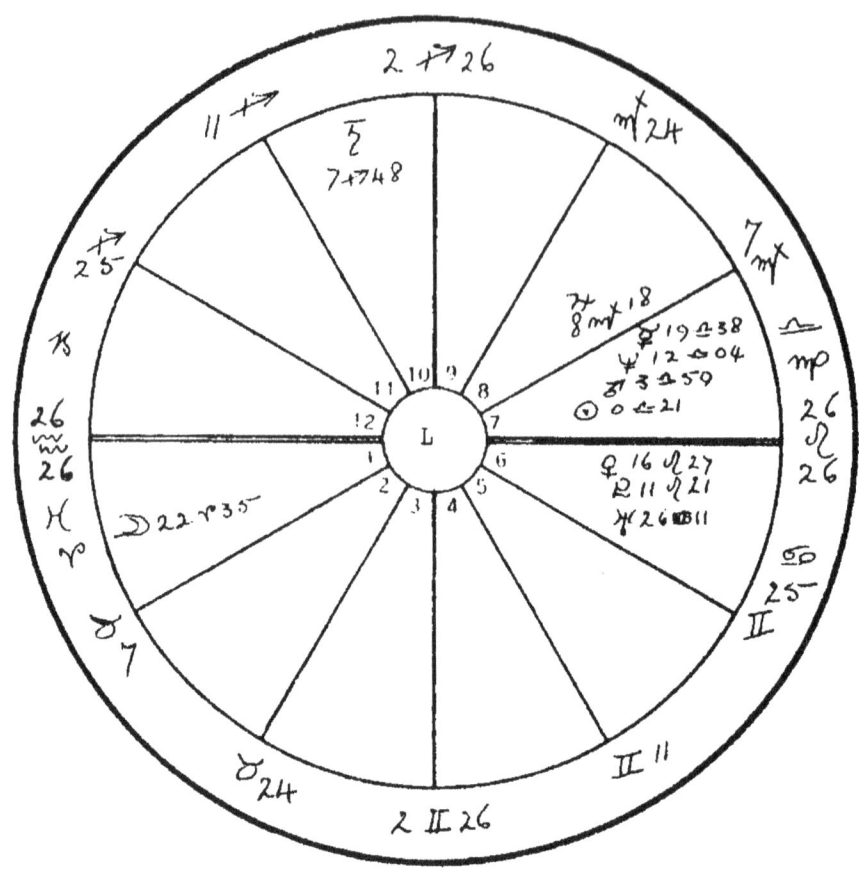

*Map L*
*Susan Walker, Solar Kinetic Return 1959*

| | | |
|---|---|---|
| Astronomical time | 14h 47m | Diurnal log .21044 |
| Moon's motion March 20 | 14 01 | Diurnal log .23357 |
| Antilog | 08 38 | .44401 |

Adding this figure to the noon position of the Moon on October 8, 1959, we have 14 Capricorn 10 in the tropical zodiac. Note: This Moon is calculated for the date of the solar return and not for March 1960.

The next step is to find at what time on March 20, 1960, the Moon will be in this tropical longitude.

| | | |
|---|---|---|
| Solar progressed Moon | 14 10 | Capricorn |
| Moon, noon March 20, 1960 | 02 49 | Capricorn |
| Difference | 11 21 | Diurnal log .32522 |
| Moon's motion March 20 | 14 10 | Diurnal log .22894 |

Antilog A.T. of solunar kinetic 19h 14m

Calculating:

| | | | |
|---|---|---|---|
| Astronomical time | 19h 14m | | |
| Acceleration | | 03 | 09 |
| S.T. noon March 20 | 23 | 52 | 04 |
| S.T. Greenwich | 19 | 09 | 13 |
| Residence West | | | 39 |
| S.T. solunar kinetic | 19 | 08 | 34 |

To be strictly accurate we should recalculate the progressed Moon using the M.S. of the above calculation (23h 56m 01s) instead of the M.S. for noon (23h 56m 01s). Here the difference is slight. Although the difference can be greater, this additional calculation will not normally be necessary.

See Map M. Saturn is on the Midheaven with the Moon. Neptune is on the Descendant. With hindsight we can interpret this as a fall (Saturn) and unconsciousness (Neptune). We could even add that Saturn is in Sagittarius, which has affinity with horses! We would not, however, claim that this map could be interpreted with such detail. It is when it is taken in connection with other maps that it has great significance.

## The Natal Quotidian Lunar Kinetic

The last of our kinetic returns is the Natal Quotidian Lunar Kinetic, N.Q.K. for short, which is based on the progressed secondary Moon. It could therefore be called the secondary lunar kinetic. It is cast for the time each lunar month when the Moon transits the position of the secondary progressed Moon. If, as we will admit, it is a little more difficult to calculate, it is well worth study as it does produce some noteworthy maps.

Our first task is to discover the approximate longitude of the progressed Moon and thus to find the day on which the Moon will transit this position. If we have kept our quotidians up to date we shall already know this position. For our example map we have already calculated the S.N.Q. and we have found that the progressed Moon on March 27 is in sidereal 14 Leo 00, which is equivalent to about 8 Virgo in the tropical zodiac.

If, however, we do not know the position of the progressed Moon for the particular date, we

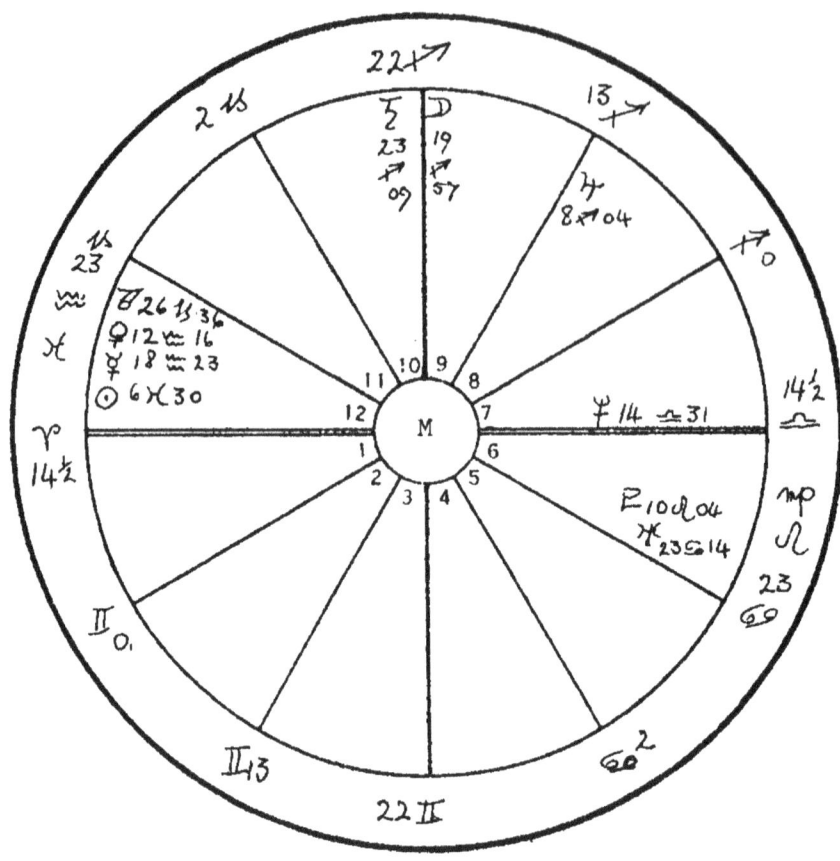

*Map M*
*Susan Walker, Solunar Kinetic Return*

must choose a date at random in the month and thus obtain the approximate position of the Moon which gives the key to the date of the N.Q.K. for that month. It may well be convenient to choose the middle of the month, in this case March 15. We will calculate by the S.N.Q. procedure the Moon for this date.

|  | Year | H | M | S |
|---|---|---|---|---|
| M.S. noon March 15, 1960 | 1959 | 23 | 32 | 22 |
| Natal M.S. corrected for age | 1949 | 13 | 06 | 11 |
| Subtract | 10 | 10 | 26 | 11 |
| Bija correction |  |  | 41 | 02 |
| Corrected age | 10 | 9 | 45 | 09 |
| Day of birth and time | 221 | 14 | 33 |  |
| Date of S.N.Q. and time | 232 | 00 | 18 | 09 |
| (October 18, 0h 18m 09s) |  |  |  |  |

For this date and time we must calculate the longitude of the Moon which will be found to be 7 Virgo 33 in the tropical zodiac. To this we must add the accrued precession between date of birth and our chosen date, i.e., 8′ 48″, making the tropical Moon for our further calculation 7 Virgo 42.

We can see from the 1960 ephemeris that the Moon transits this position on March 11/12. We need to know the position of the progressed Moon on this date which is three and a half days before the trial date of March 15. The progressed Moon moves on an average about two minutes a day. We must therefore deduct seven minutes from the longitude of the progressed Moon which we have found for March 15. This makes the progressed Moon for the date of the N.Q.K. 7 Virgo 35. We shall not normally need greater accuracy than this. If we do we must recalculate the Moon for March 12, the date of the N.Q.K.

We now have to calculate an ordinary lunar return for a Moon of 7 Virgo 35 tropical.

| Moon's position | 07 35 | Virgo |
|---|---|---|
| Moon noon March 11 | 28 30 | Leo |
| Difference | 09 05 | Diurnal log .42197 |
| Moon's motion March 11 | 12 59 | Diurnal log .26683 |
| Antilog 16h 47m |  | .15514 |

We will calculate this map.

|  | H M S |
|---|---|
| A.T. of N.Q.K. | 16 47 |
| Acceleration | 02 45 |
| S.T. March 11 | 23 16 35 |
| S.T. Greenwich | 16 06 20 |
| Residence West | 39 |
| S.T. of N.Q.K. | 16 05 41 |

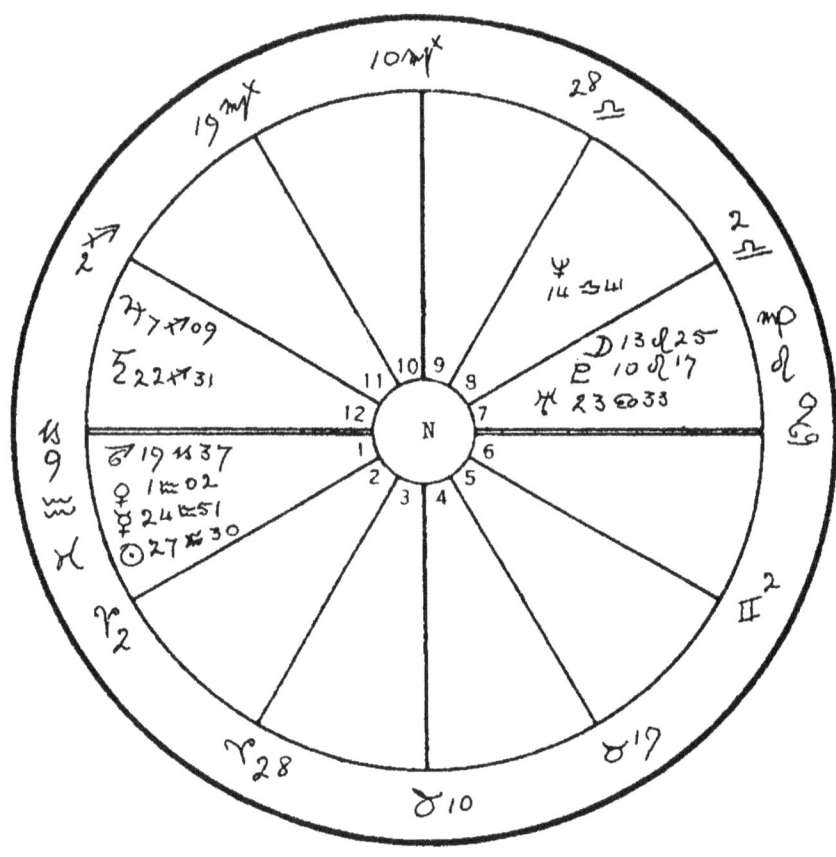

*Map N*
*Susan Walker, Natal Quotidian Kinetic Return*

See Map N. Mars rises opposite Uranus which is conjunct natal Pluto and Mars. Note that this map is 15 days before the event on March 27. It is probable that these maps progress but we have not yet found the correct rate for the progression of the angles. It does seem probable that the closer the planets are to the angles the more closely will the event follow the date of the map. The aspects here are eminently suitable for an accident and do involve disturbing the harmony of the life.

## Chapter XVII

# Mundane Astrology

This chapter is not intended to be a treatise on mundane nor political astrology. We shall only deal with the methods based on the sidereal zodiac which have been found to be effective. For a comprehensive book on the methods hitherto used in mundane astrology, the reader is referred to *An Introduction to Political Astrology* by C.E.O. Carter.

It has long been the custom in this branch of astrology to consider maps drawn for the time of the entry of the Sun into the cardinal signs: Aries, Cancer, Libra and Capricorn. Of these, the Aries ingress was by tradition considered the most important and possibly to be thought of as "the map of the year." Led by Carter, astrologers have begun to consider the Capricorn as the prime ingress.

It was also Carter who suggested that if the sidereal zodiac were valid, maps for the entry of the Sun into the constellations of Aries, Cancer, Libra and Capricorn would be of importance. This suggestion was followed up by Garth Allen, who in an extensive statistical investigation found that these sidereal ingresses were not only valid but of the highest significance. This opinion has been fully confirmed by other investigators in recent years. Garth Allen eventually arrived at the conclusion that the Capricorn sidereal ingress was of primary importance, followed in rank by that of Cancer; Aries and Libra, whilst having some significance, could be considered of lesser importance.

These sidereal ingresses differ completely from their tropical counterparts, Whilst, for example, the Capricorn tropical ingress is nonnally on December 21 of each year, the corresponding sidereal ingress will be cast for January 14/15, a difference of some 24 days. The angles and the positions of the planets will be different.

The accuracy of these ingresses depends directly on the correctness of the *ayanamsa* or difference in longitude between the two zodiacs. An inaccuracy of one minute in the *ayanamsa* will result in an alteration of the M.C. by about six degrees. These maps are therefore of considerable importance in judging the accuracy of the Fagan-Allen *ayanamsas.* As a result of a statistical study of mundane maps in the sidereal zodiac, Allen corrected Fagan's hypsomatic *ayanamsa* by 6' 05".

These ingresses may be said to set the cosmic atmosphere of the period for which the ingress is valid, that of Capricorn having influence throughout the year. The extent to which a country or an individual leader responds to this cosmic atmosphere must depend on the natal map of the solar return of that country or leader. The doctrine of subsumption is fully justified in mundane astrology. Where possible, therefore, we must consider the sidereal ingress as well as the natal and solar return maps of the country or leader concerned. Often, two or more countries are involved in a particular situation, necessitating a study of other maps. When we realize that in addition to ingresses we should study progressions and also lunar ingresses, it will be seen that the task is difficult and demands time and energy.

We shall not deal with new moon maps which are so often used, being similar in either zodiac, but we express the opinion that they have not the same value as ingresses of national maps. As astrologers we must admit that the birth map should show what is happening to a country and should be the primary consideration in judging possible events. Unfortunately, there is a lack of reliable information on the date and time of national maps. Often this is completely unknown, often (as with the national map of the United States) there are rival maps in existence. The way of the mundane astrologer is indeed hard and for this reason alone one can forgive the lack of success in this branch of our art.

## Sidereal Solar Ingresses

We shall now consider the calculation of sidereal solar ingresses. These are identical with a solar return to 0 degrees of the constellation and present little difficulty when we are using a sidereal ephemeris. Indeed, Stahl's solunar ephemerides give the time for the entry of the Sun into all constellations.

If we are using a tropical ephemeris we first have to determine the degree of the tropical zodiac which, on the date of the ingress, corresponds to zero degrees of the constellation. Using a tropical ephemeris we shall calculate the Capricorn sidereal solar ingress for 1965 for London.

The *ayanamsa* for the date of the Capricorn ingress for 1965 is 24° 14' 51". This is obtained by deducting the Synetic Vernal Point for January 14, 1965, which is given in Stahl's *Ephemeris of the Vernal Point* from 30 degrees, and also in most tropical ephemerides. The tropical longitude to which the Sun returns for the sidereal ingress is therefore Capricorn 24° 14' 53.2". To calculate this figure we proceed as for a solar return.

| | | |
|---|---|---|
| Ingress tropical longitude | 24 14 05 | |
| Sun's trop. long. noon Jan. 14 | 24 07 36 | |
| Difference | 07 15 | Ternary log 1.39493 |
| Sun's motion Jan. 14/15 | 01 01 05 | Ternary log .4693 |
| Diurnal antilog 2h 5m | | .92558 |

Stahl in his solunar ephemeris for 1965 gives 14h 51m 03s U.T. for the ingress which is the same time as we have found by using a tropical ephemeris. If you are using a sidereal ephemeris you will naturally work from the Sun in 0 Capricorn.

These ingresses can be progressed by either the P.S.S.R. or the S.Q. rate as explained in Chapters X and XII. Progressions will bring the planets to the angles in turn, showing the local influence in force.

If there are important conjunctions or oppositions in the ingress, the time when these come to the angles will be critical. It will be found that at different localities two planets may simultaneously come to adjacent angles, a very important formation. This will only apply to a particular latitude as the rising and setting times of these planets will differ with the latitude.

In spite of the value of these ingresses we hold that it is the national map and its returns which act as the trigger to set off the cosmic action. Unfortunately we are not in possession of many important national maps. This is a grave handicap to the mundane astrologer and renders his task more difficult.

It has been found that the coincidence of planets in the ingress with personal planets in our own maps may tend to induce events of the nature of the planets concerned.

## Sidereal Lunar Ingresses

Solar ingresses give the cosmic atmosphere of the year or of the quarter. Lunar ingresses of which that of Capricorn is probably the most important set the atmosphere of the month. In addition to casting the Capricorn lunar ingress we would advise casting that of Cancer. If this throws up an important figure it will have an effect. Otherwise the Capricorn lunar ingress lasts the whole month. We have occasionally found an Aries or Libra lunar ingress of value. The key is probably that a striking figure for any of these ingresses will take effect.

These ingresses are calculated exactly as a lunar return. If we are using a tropical ephemeris we must find the corresponding tropical position of the Moon as we did for the solar ingress, by adding the *ayanamsa,* bringing the ingress tropical Moon for February 27, the day of an ingress, to Capricorn 24° 14′ 57″.

We will calculate this ingress using a sidereal ephemeris and zero degrees sidereal Capricorn.

| | | |
|---|---|---|
| Moon's required longitude | 00 00 00 | Capricorn |
| Moon 6h U.T. Feb. 27 | <u>27 42 41</u> | Sagittarius |
| Difference | 02 17 19 | 6h log .41858 |
| Moon's motion 6 hours | 02 57 45 | 6h log <u>.30649</u> |
| 6h antilog is 4h 38m 07s | | .11209 |

Adding to this figure the 0600 hours U.T. from which we are working we obtain 10h 38m 07s as the U.T. of the lunar return. This agrees with the figure for the U.T. given in Stahl's sidereal ephemeris. In this example we have interpolated, but for lunar ingresses this is not normally necessary, it being sufficient to work to the nearest minute.

## Map Sections

In the following sections we include all the maps of which the calculation has been explained in this book. We recommend that the student should study them as a whole. It is our belief that important events in the life are shown on more than one map.

In this series it will be found that the event, often expressed in different symbolism, will be found in each map. Individual maps, however, will show different features of the event. It will be seen that in some the Mars-Uranus opposition is strongly indicated whilst in others the Saturn is strong; in still others Neptune. We note also the continual presence of the preserver, Jupiter.

We feel that by considering these maps together we can arrive at a closer approximation to the actual event than we could do from one map. The study of more than one map will strengthen our ability to forecast actual events. We have not ventured on any rectification. Some may wish to do so after a study of the maps.

It seems probable that any sensitive point in a map, such as its solar or natal position can form the basis for a return map. With the slower planets the accuracy given in the ephemeris is not great enough for really accurate maps for which we have to turn to the nautical almanacs. The research student may care to experiment with a map for the return of Mars to its natal position.

Maps are drawn by the Campanus system of house division.

Students are advised to redraw them by their favourite system, of which unfortunately there are many.

In the maps we shall mark planets as follows:
Natal planets in black with N.
Transiting planets in red with T.
[Ed. Note: The maps are placed in their respective chapters.]

# Chapter XVIII

# The Art of Interpretation

## The Natus

The true art of the interpretation of a birth horoscope lies in the selection between major and minor factors in the map and the subsequent synthesis of these factors into a coherent whole. If we merely extract from our knowledge or from textbooks the apparent meaning of individual factors without regard to the individual factors and their relative importance, we shall mislead ourselves and the native, as it is customary to call the subject of the geniture under consideration. The more difficult task is the synthesis, and for the accomplishment of this we must call upon all our powers of experience, knowledge and intuition. We shall be greatly aided if we can fix firmly the most important features of the map as these will colour the whole.

Before proceeding to state which in our opinion are the major factors in a horoscope we must state our opinion on certain theories which are commonly accepted.

## House Division

According to the theory of house division, a horoscope is divided into a number of spaces or houses, each of which has dominion over different aspects of the activities of a life. Nowadays the number of houses is usually twelve, the *dodekatopos,* the houses being enumerated in a counterclockwise direction. Originally the mundane sphere was divided into eight equal spaces which ran clockwise so that the first house or space (the house of life) tallied with the temporal hours 6 a.m. to 9 a.m., whilst the last or eighth house (the house of death) synchronised with the temporal hours from 3 a.m. to 6 a.m. For the full description of this *oktopopos,* as this system is called, see *SPICA,* Volume III, No.2. When the twelve-hour system was universally adopted, the dominions assigned to the houses of the eight-fold framework remained unaltered. Thus the second house (means of livelihood and money), which in the *oktopopos* corresponds with 9 a.m. to 12 noon, usually the busiest hours of the day, in the twelve-house system tallied with 2 a.m. to 4 a.m., the hours of slumber. If houses are based on the temporal hours, this is an absurdity. In the interpretation of the horoscope of Wallenstein, Johann Kepler, the distinguished astronomer and astrologer, abandoned all methods of intetpretation based on houses (and incidentally the so-called ruling planets), dismissing them as mere superstition and unworthy of consideration.

We must admit that if there are no houses our powers of interpretation of a horoscope are decreased as we cannot specify which particular planet or planets have rule over a particular aspect of the activities of life. If we do not accept houses we must accept this restriction and rely on other methods to produce a truer, if shorter, picture of the native. We will confess that at the present moment of time we remain agnostic as to the value of houses in a nativity.

If houses there be, and students may well wish to experiment with them, there remains a wide variety of choice. It is indeed said that there are 51 different house systems! Of these the best known are those of Placidus, Campanus, Regiomontanus, the Equal House systems (which are strictly not mundane divisions of the sphere but zodiacal) and the recently introduced Topocentric system of Nelson Page and Polich, which produces cusps which are very close to those of Placidus; and the Birthplace house system of Dr. Walter Koch. Regiomontanus has fallen out of fashion. Placidus does not work in high latitudes (here all systems run into difficulties). The Campanian system is well known, and the Koch and the Topocentric systems have been fully described in *SPICA*.

## Power and the Angles

Tradition and personal experience alike have demonstrated that when a celestial body is mundanely, i.e., bodily, on an angle (Ascendant, Descendant, M.C. or I.C.), it exercises for weal or woe its maximum power. The Ascendant or rising degree, anciently referred to as the *horoscopus* was known as the Point of Sunrise. Opposite to it was the Descendant, Point of Sunset, or *dysis*. The Egyptians viewed this point as the entrance to the underworld. The M.C. or Midheaven is that point of the ecliptic which culminates due south at any given time. Its opposite point or I.C. (the antimeridian) is always due north.

Planets found in the vicinity of any of these four angles (on either side of the angle) are said to be in the immediate foreground. Here their influence is most powerful and can colour the whole interpretation of the horoscope.

## The Inactive Places

We must now consider the concept of the inactive places in a horoscope. It may be held that if planets exercise their maximum power on the angles, it would follow that they are at their weakest when situated midway between any adjacent pair of angles. Such a position of inactivity was recognised in remote antiquity. The Greeks call this position *argos topos* and the Romans *locus piger,* both terms meaning an inactive or lazy place. Although in most house systems the angles are identical, these midway positions will vary in accordance with the house system used.

Garth Allen and his scientific coworkers appear to have solved the problem of the location of these inactive places by their statistical analysis of 49,576 samples of excess rainfall in the United States. In this experiment Jupiter on an angle in lunar returns tallied with excess rainfall whereas Jupiter in these return maps when on the midway point tallied with minimum rainfall. In this analysis the midpoints were calculated on the prime vertical or the system of Campanus. This is conclusive evidence in favour of Campanus at least as regards the location of the inactive spaces. If there are houses it might well be held that this is also evidence in favour of a Campanian system of house division.

The test of any house system, either in nativity or in return maps, should be whether, analogous to the admitted power of planets on angles, a planet has any special strength when on an intermediate cusp in terms of the alleged functions of that house. Has a planet, for example, on the third house cusp any particular strength in terms of third house activities? So far this has not been demonstrated to our satisfaction. We remain open to conviction.

## Rulers of Houses

It has been considered in the past that a house in a map had as its ruler the planet ruling the sign on its cusp. Thus if Gemini were on the cusp of the third house its house ruler would be Mercury and it was by the condition and aspects of Mercury in the horoscope that the affairs of the third house would be judged. In addition any planets situated in the house concerned must be considered. This technique of house rulers is particularly well developed in horary astrology.

There are considerable difficulties in accepting this theory of house rulership. Even if we accept the modern theory of rulership by assigning Uranus to Aquarius, Neptune to Pisces and Pluto to Scorpio, or at any rate to some constellation, as opinion on these rulerships is not fixed, we are left with Mercury and Venus each ruling two constellations. As the same constellation may be, even in moderate latitudes, on the cusp of no less than three houses, any aspect between these planets may involve the attributes of no less than five houses. Such a scheme is of no practical value in the delineation of a horoscope. With Sagittarius on the eleventh and twelfth house cusps it seems absurd to consider Jupiter as representing both our friends (eleventh) and our secret enemies (twelfth).

We further hold that such a system distorts the pure meaning of the planets. We hold that Venus always remains Venus, with the attributes of Venus. Under any house system Venus as a house ruler might be the significator of violent death. It is for these and other reasons that we reject house rulership as having no practical value in the astrological delineation of a nativity.

## General Principles of Interpretation

Although the preceding paragraphs were written as applying to the natus, they also generally apply to progressed maps and to solar returns with their progressions and to lunar returns. When an observation applies only to one class of map it will be so stated.

Interpretation is mainly based on the relative positions of the planetary bodies in relation to the foreground and background. Should the benefics be on the angles and the malefics in the background the chart may be deemed to be highly fortunate. It will be otherwise if these positions are reversed. Main attention should therefore be directed to planets near the angles and near the inactive places. Planets in zodiacal square to the angles are also important, possibly because they are then at the midpoint between opposite angles.

## Configurations (Aspects)

In the practice of sidereal astrology, far and away the most powerful aspects are those compatible with the four angles, the conjunction, opposition and the square. These are the principal aspects to which our attention should be directed. We reject the so-called minor aspects, particularly in return maps. Even the popular trine is of doubtful value.

It is of great importance to recognise that the quality of an aspect depends on the innate nature of the planets involved in the configuration and not on the angular distance between them. Thus a square between benefics is definitely to be regarded as benefic. Sun square Jupiter is potent for good.

## Paranatellonta

When two or more planets are simultaneously on the same, adjacent or opposite angles they are said to be in *paranatellonta*. This is the most powerful of all configurations.

Natal planets may enjoy no mutual zodiacal aspect but may be in *paranatellonta* at certain times of the day. To find whether planets are in this formation the student is referred to a section of this book. Such configurations are particularly important when they fall on the angles of a return map whether cast for the birthplace or for the place of residence. A change of residence can alter the formation of *paranatellonta* .

## The Fallacy of "Thingish" Thought

Planets including the luminaries denote a state of consciousness or of awareness, but not things or persons. The Sun used to be regarded as representing the father or the monarch, the Moon the mother, Saturn the miser or the workhouse, and so on. We now know that Jupiter represents a state of elation or joy which may be the sequel to any number of diversified happenings, the receipt of money, promotion, increased status or preservation from danger. It could also arise from the death of an unwanted person. Everything depends on the psychological makeup of the native. All that an astrologer can truthfully predict is that, with Jupiter in the foreground, the native will be elated and happy. If he is sufficiently venturesome as to prophesy the cause of the elation, he deserts astrology for mere speculation.

Similarly, with Mars in the foreground there is a feeling of acute discomfort if not pain. With Saturn a feeling of neglect, loneliness and disappointment. Later we shall deal with the intrinsic effects of all the planets.

## The Seat of Consciousness

The seat of awareness for oneself as a distinct and separate consciousness which recognises itself as the "I," the "Me" and the "Mine," which is acutely aware of physical and psychic pleasure and pain, lies at the intersection of the planes of the meridian and horizon, namely at the centre of Earth itself. Psychologists call this the "psychological centre of gravity."

For astrological purposes, man may be considered as living geocentrically; that is, at the centre of Earth. This is why transits of the malefics to any one of the angles or directions of the angles to the malefics are accompanied by an awareness of acute suffering, whilst those of the benefics give intense pleasure. The more remote from the angles are the malefics or benefics the less the awareness of suffering or of pleasure will be. The native will be totally unaware of the most baneful configurations of the heavens should they fall in or near the inactive places.

## The Seat of the Ego

The Sun, significator of ambition and the thirst for fame and recognition, is usually held to be the symbol of the Ego or Higher Self; its zodiacal position and configurations with the planets determine the characteristics and conditioning of the Ego. As the Sun is in the centre of its own system it cannot actually be in any constellation or in configuration with any planet. It therefore has no characteristics nor can it be conditioned in any way. When we state that on November 30, 1874, the Sun was in the constellation Scorpio 15° 10′ 17″, we actually mean that the Earth was in the same degree, minute and second of the opposite constellation, Taurus. The longitude of the Sun is only apparent. The Ego is not symbolised by the Sun but by Earth itself, which, viewed geocentrically, is reflected in the mirror of the solar disc.

Being a satellite of Earth, the Moon also partakes in this awareness of self and others as separate consciousnesses. In Hindu astrology, the *janma lagna* (Ascendant) and the *janma rasi* (Moon) are both taken as denoting the native. Viewed heliocentrically from the Sun, the Moon has precisely the same longitudes as Earth. In all cases, therefore, the real seat of the Ego is denoted by the Earth on which we live, move and have our being.

## Accidents and Incidents

Events in astrology are classified as being either accidents or incidents or sometimes a mixture of both. Accidents are caused by transits whilst incidents proceed from primary or secondary direction. A mixture of both occurs when a planet transits a progressed significator. The gradual transformation of the small acorn into the fully grown tree can be said to be incidental to the acorn for it held within itself the promise of the future timber. But the oak can be felled by the axe or struck by lightning, events which are not innate in the acorn but external to it.

Such events are known as accidents and their cause must be linked with planets in transit. The accidental death of the infirm is usually caused by transit over a progressed significator.

If from the appearance of an eclipse an astrologer successfully predicts an earthquake that kills thousands, the astrological cause of the earthquake is obviously the eclipse, an "accident." It would be useless to search the directions of a victim for the cause of death. Yet astrologers have been doing this for centuries.

## Significators and Promittors

The planets, including the luminaries, can be considered as either significators or promittors. In a mutual configuration one planet is usually taken as the significator and the other as promittor. The mind is signified by Mercury and its expression (but not its depth) is denoted by the constellation Mercury is in and the aspects which it makes with the other planets, which here act as promittors. For instance, should Mercury be in conjunction with Venus at birth, the mind will normally express itself in a gracious, if not poetic, way, being agreeable in conversation with all, as befits Venus. Here Mercury is the significator and Venus the promittor.

On the other hand, Venus is the significator of the affections. It signifies the people, things and places that give one intense pleasure and that one wishes to return to time and again.

Should Venus be configured at birth with Mercury, the native will have a happy childhood, later delighting in memories of his school days. Loving his mentors, learning will come easily to him and he will have a fondness for travel and literature. Should Venus, however, be configured with Mars and Saturn acting in consort, the native may take a pleasure in things that are vile and cruel, and tend to eschew the decencies of life.

## Transits to the Outer Planets

Unless they are in the immediate foreground, transits to the outermost planets, Uranus, Neptune and Pluto, need not be considered. Such transits affect generally everyone born during the same year as the native. This is because their yearly motion is so slow that their positions will only alter by a degree or so during this period.

## The Physical Body and the Angles

The physical body with its sensitivity to pleasure and pain is signified by the four angles but especially by the *horoscopus* or the degree of the zodiac that was crossing the Eastern horizon at the moment of his birth. Often it will be found that one or other of the four angles of the native interchange with those of one of his parents or with those of his children, even to the precise degree. This can be useful in rectification. The Ascendant that rises at birth modified by the constellations which hold the Sun and Moon together with the configurations to other natal planets determine the signature or personal appearance of the native.

When the angles of the various return maps are directed to the benefics the native will enjoy good health or, if ill, will recover. If they are directed to the malefics he will be in acute or chronic discomfiture or suffer ill health. Transits over the angles have the same effect but are less enduring. In particular that of Mars is prone to cause influenza and such like epidemics. The final dissolution usually takes place under a malefic bombardment of the angles.

Pleasant or otherwise, all bodily sensations are felt via the angles. Happenings that are not recognised by the physical senses, such as mental abstractions and the like, will only be shown in the foreground should they occasion some physical disturbance. Otherwise they will be comprehended through transits to the appropriate signiflcaror, The evolution of a scheme for making money will not necessarily be shown by directions or transits affecting the angles; they may be shown by directions or transits to the natal or progressed Jupiter.

## The Influencs of the Sun and Moon Contrasted

As most human relationships are dominated by the luminaries it will be wise to consider them in some detail in order to help our intetpretation. The Sun person is one who has that luminary dominant at birth or who has it configured with the Moon or other planet in another geniture. The same applies to the Moon person. The dualism between the positive Sun and the negative Moon can be seen in every walk of life, in the relationship between the king and the commoner, the sergeant and the private, the mistress and the maid. Although generally the Sun is held to symbolise the male and the Moon the female, this is not always true and quite frequently the symbolism is reversed. It would appear that Moon people are considerably in excess of Sun people. This appears to be in accord with natural law for we find this in the animal kingdom—but for some unknown reason not in that of insects—one bull to a herd of cows, irrespective of the species.

Whilst the Sun identifies itself with its creations, its achievements and its political life, what it stands for, the Moon identifies itself with its own personality, its appearance, popularity and its health. The Moon represents the image of the native in movement; the image that catches the public eye; his appearance as seen on the hustings; the floor of the house, the stage, the television screen and in the press. The Sun depicts him in the closet of his workshop; the Moon as he parades before his viewers in the make and motley of pretence and make-belief. The Sun reveals us as we are, the Moon as we would like to be. These dual images are often widely contradictory. The purpose of most biographers is to tear away the masquerade so that the true individual can be revealed.

One who has the Moon configured with the benefics will outwardly appear to be the most charmalefics he could be a monster at heart. On the other hand, one can be cursed with the disagreeable manner of the afflicted Moon and yet have the heart of gold of the Sun aspected by the benefics. We have to decide which of these twin natures has the upper hand and this depends in no small measure on the luminary which is elevated (near the M.C.) or closer to an angle.

The Sun is the creator, the Moon the executant. The Moon may be the greatest singer in the world but it is the Sun who writes the songs; the Moon may be the best dressed woman in society but as always it is the Sun that designed the gown. Overnight the Moon may become famous but fame comes to the Sun more meagerly and more tardily and indeed often posthumously. Nevertheless the Sun enjoys the greater satisfaction. Great indeed is his pride in achievement.

## The Sun

The Sun (actually the Earth) signifies the vital core of our being, the man or woman as he is actually at heart and as only his wife, children and his intimate associates see him. If he is born at local sunrise, noon, sunset, or even midnight, when the Sun will be in the foreground, he will tend to forge a path for himself in life as he itches to rule and command others. If, however, he is born when the Sun is remote from the angles these, qualities will not be obvious and may even be absent.

If the natal Sun be in the foreground and the Moon in the background the native will be a self-made man, determined and possibly ruthless. This is especially noticeable when the Sun is in one of the "foundation" constellations, Scorpio, Aquarius, Taurus or Leo, when he may heed no council other than his own. Should the Moon be angular especially in the weak constellations, Sagittarius, Pisces, Gemini or VIrgo, and the Sun cadent, the native will be weak, having little stamina and swayed by the opinions of others.

**The Sun as Significator**

The Sun is the source of life and manifests itself physically as vitality and psychologically as the quest for fame. It is the seat of the intelligence and its interests are conditioned by the constellation it was in at birth and with its aspects on that date. For example, should the Sun be in the constellation Aries at birth the native will show a strong interest in power politics and the control and management of others. Should it be in the meek and considerate Taurus, the pursuit of wisdom and knowledge for its own sake will be his life concern. In Leo there will be the feeling of innate superiority possibly finding its outlet in the study of history, castles and family trees. The peacemakers of the world will be found with the Sun in Libra, the greatest warriors with Scorpio whilst Pisces claims those who delight in make-believe such as actors. This question has been fully discussed in *The Symbolism of the Constellations*.

**The Sun Configured with Mercury**

These natives will be slim, nimble, boyish in build, highly strung, restless, garrulous, travelling a good deal and inclined to business generally. They will be the worrying kind and excel at mathematics or calculations.

**The Sun Configured with Venus**

The native will have a pleasing appearance, be graceful in his movements, gentle in speech and usually loved by all. He is in love with beauty and the arts and is a favourite of the fair sex when a male.

**The Sun Configured with Mars**

This is a vigorous formation and the native will not be averse to pleasures of the senses. He will be active and energetic and have a sound constitution with reserves of energy.

**The Sun Configured with Jupiter**

If well-placed in the foreground the native may be fortunately placed in life. He may well have the benefits of a good heritage. He may have aspirations for the cultural side of life and strive for the professions. He will fell at ease in circles which revere the "old school tie." With Jupiter acting in its role of "preserver" he will be fortunate amongst men and will find a way out of difficulties.

**The Sun Configured with Saturn**

Here the native will be inclined to be of the serious type and drawn to philosophy and other serious studies. Naturally skeptical, he demands adequate experimental proof before adopting a thesis as true. Inclined to eschew frivolities and living an abstemious life, he usually manages to live to a ripe old age with all his faculties intact.

**The Sun Configured with Uranus**

These Sun-Uranus folk can be quite unique and exciting in their way. They are so unexpectedly and refreshingly novel in all they do that those who come before the public often strike the headlines and cause a public sensation. As Uranus is the promittor of inspiration they seem to seize the right moment to do the right thing and therefore excel in politics, adventure, sport and science.

**The Sun Configured with Neptune**

These people are often gifted with large doe-like and expressive eyes. They tend to live, as artists, in a world of their own making, a world of fantasia, of drama, music, dance and make-believe, divorced from the harsh world of reality. If compelled to live in such a world, as most are, they like to translate it into art. Having very abnormal and sensitive imaginations they are temperamental and are quick to "blow their top." Essentially escapists, there is a danger of addiction to drugs or drink as they are fascinated by temptation. They are the habitues of the entertainment world from grand opera to pop music.

**The Sun Configured with Pluto**

Sun-Pluto folk are apt to be the "odd men out" of society. Feeling this, some prefer to live in isolation. They do not fit in well with community life. A lack of warmth in human relationships makes them the separatists they are. This tendency can be dangerous and lead to antisocial activities. It can also manifest as outstanding ability, unique in its way, which can lead to a commanding position. Sun-Pluto people can rank among the great class of men of genius.

**Solar Progressions and Directions**

*Note: These descriptions of the progressed aspects will generally apply to aspects in solar and lunar return maps but only when one of the planets is angular. If neither is angular they will be unimportant and can be disregarded.*

***To Moon***: Fundamental changes in the native's menage usually take place when the progressed or regressed Sun is configured with the natal Moon. These can arise from varying circumstances such as the death of a parent, a change of occupation, a removal and so forth. In a male geniture it frequently means that at this time a woman comes to live in the domicile and takes over the management. It thus frequently indicates marriage. At this time the native usually becomes more self-conscious especially in his relationship with the opposite sex.

***To Mercury***: Here there can only be the conjunction which must occur before his 28th year. Usually it denotes the awakening of the mind to mental pursuits, often at the age when the native goes to school. If this aspect matures when he is adult he will at that time take a deeper interest in mental pursuits, including sometimes astronomy and astrology. He could also enter into employment.

***To Venus***: The progressed or regressed Sun must form its conjunction with the natal Venus before the 48th year. To the progressed Venus it can be later. Its conjunction with the natal Venus normally coincides with the period when the native becomes sensitive to beauty and craves for friendship and close relationship with others. Hence he will make friends, fall in love or become interested in the arts or music. At this time he becomes more conscious of his appearance and smartens his wardrobe. This is a very happy period for the native.

***To Mars***: When the progressed Sun forms a configuration with Mars, natal or progressed, the native becomes acutely conscious of his sex nature. This may get out of control and wild oats may be sown. It is a time when escapades may not please his seniors. He will become more boisterous and out of hand. There is a superfluous energy which he may seek to work off in vigorous games. Knowing little fear he is capable of acts of daring. This period may lead to a greater interest in mechanical things or to joining one of the armed services.

***To Jupiter***: We can expect the most successful period of one's life when the progressed or regressed Sun is configured with Jupiter. This is the time that, provided only that an effort is made, success will come to the native. At college he will attain his degree, prizes will be won in sport and he will prosper in business or in his profession. Under this direction reputations are made and fortunes laid.

***To Saturn***: The solar progression to Saturn synchronises with the most disappointing periods of one's life, the effects of which may leave a scar. Under this progression the native may fail to pass a test, he may be passed over for promotion or rejected at an interview. He may lose his job. If a politician, he may lose an election. It is not a fortunate time for undertakings. It is a period of depression from which it may take time to recover. Under its influence the native is fearful, overly cautious and envious of the success of others because his pride has been hurt.

***To Uranus***: This can be a period of illumination when light can break through the hardened set condition of the mind. This is the moment for the flash of genius to appear, if the native is capable of it. This progression tallies with the most inspired periods of the life when we can set ourselves free from the traditional. Many at this time break with custom and do unexpected things, and if a public figure, may well hit the headlines. He will be bent on discovering the world and exults in adventures. His inventive talent will express itself in unorthodox ways. It is a time of change.

***To Neptune***: Under Neptunian influence the native's evaluation of himself increases but is largely fictitious. He is unable to see himself clearly. He may become unduly sensitive to the opinions of others. He may be the butt of ridicule and suffer severely at the hands of others in his surroundings. His overwrought imagination enhances his fears. He becomes easily agitated, worried and flurried. Under the Neptunian influence, guilt may carry the stigma of shame or disgrace especially if Saturn also comes into the picture. The craving for sensation will be enhanced and temptation will be put in his path which he will find difficult to resist. He will dwell in a world of fantasy to the detriment of clear thinking and bad effect on his practical work.

***To Pluto***: The solar direction to Pluto marks the beginning or the end of a stage in life. It can begin a new phase with success or end one with failure. Under this configuration the marriage tie may be broken and couples parted. Under it children leave home and go out into the world to fend for themselves. It is responsible for the death of parents and the loss of friends. One can feel separate from others and therefore in some cases antisocial. The native may be at war with others and in mundane maps it is a promittor of actual warfare. No other planet changes the status quo as does Pluto.

***The Moon***: According to ancient tradition the Moon held sway over the four bodily humours: blood, phlegm, choler and melancholy. Of these humours the one in ascendancy determined the quality of the mind. Reacting to every movement and challenge in one's environment and sensitive to the effects of food and drink, the condition of one's stomach can drastically determine one's humours. It was the author of the *Tetrabiblos* who said that the Moon decides the nature of the irrational soul. Like the restless sea, it is, as it were, easily becalmed and just as easily lashed into fury by every wind that blows. It is, however, incapable of any initiative of its own. How we walk, talk, eat, sleep, laugh and cry are its business. It is responsible for our behaviour, our mannerisms and our idiosyncrasies. Its zodiacal location determines our likes and dislikes. It fashions our emotions, feelings and imagination, our lust for sensation and our hysterical outbursts.

Anciently the Moon was considered the cause of lunacy. At its door can be laid most of the maladies which affect the soul. Classical and medieval authors describe those who have the

Moon dignified at birth and well placed as being soft, tender creatures, timorous and easily frightened and as easily influenced. They live on their feelings, and are incapable of independent action. They can be work-shy and quite contented to live carelessly. These are perhaps extreme cases but they show the tendencies of an afflicted Moon.

When the native's Sun is configured with another's Moon he tends to overlord that person and to push him about. He tells his lunar counterpart what to do and expects him or her to do it. The lunar person would never think of going against his wishes. Yet this is one of the most successful interchanges for partnership, especially that of marriage.

### The Moon in Natal Configuration

*With Mercury*: The native is endowed with considerable mental acumen, especially when the Moon is in opposition. Here the mental output will be great and the capacity to imbibe knowledge prodigious. Not infrequently this configuration is the diathesis of genius. An excellent memory is accompanied by a remarkable linguistic ability. He will excel in all branches of learning. He is inclined to be restless and is often afflicted with the "wanderlust" and therefore usually manages to travel extensively. It is an aspect of common sense, a valuable commodity for success.

*With Venus*: Complete is the concord between "hand" and "heart" when the Moon is configured with Venus in the geniture. One of the most pleasant of testimonies, it bestows grace and charm, a pleasing smile and a melodious voice. Thus blessed the native makes friends with great facility and is warmly welcomed wherever he goes. A successful lover, his adventures in this direction may be many. "Matinee idols" may have this configuration and some are a little effeminate. Yet they always have their coterie of admirers.

*With Mars*: When thus configured, natives "rush in where angels fear to tread." Not knowing the meaning of shyness they lead the world. Exceptionally intelligent and quick on the uptake, they are always in the vanguard, shepherding others and leading them into the fold. Immediately sizing up a situation, they act without counting the cost and may get their fingers burned. They are outspoken and inclined to put awkward questions to a lecturer. At school they are "enfants terribles" and invariably find themselves in trouble. Their precipitancy all too frequently lands them in difficulties but they are irrepressible.

*With Jupiter*: Whilst Neptune seems to denote quantity, Jupiter symbolises quality. Those who have the Moon configured at birth with the greatest of the benefics aspire to the best things of life, and like to surround themselves with them. They like to move in the best circles however humbly they themselves may be born, to take of the best of food and drink and to attend good schools. The height of their ambition would be to be a politician, if not a statesman. Others prefer advancement in the church or in the professions or in academic life.

They impress by their education, culture, seeming sagacity, tact, diplomacy, optimism and good humour. This latter trait could be hilarious if Jupiter is also configured with Mars, which can add a touch of coarseness. These people usually succeed in life not only because of their qualifications but because they manage to live respectably and decorously, doing all things in moderation.

*With Saturn*: Because those who have this configuration at birth tend to suffer from some chronic disability of that part of the body which comes under the dominion of the constellation holding the Moon, they tend to be depressed, melancholy, morbid, pessimistic, laborious, ponderous in thought, absent-minded, hesitant in speech and given to philosophic brooding. These qualities do not make for success or popular appeal. They know hardship, frustration and even failure and poverty. In constant fear of tomorrow they clutch at money coming their way and tend to hoard it. There is a fear of insecurity and on account of this they may feel resentment. Their work tends to keep them in the background. If Saturn is configured with Pluto the life of an anchorite would make strong appeal to some.

*With Uranus*: In contradistinction to Saturn, the significator of all things that are stale, hoary, traditional, Uranus betokens the eternal spring of youth, the quality of freshness, newness, the original and the yet untried. Ideas that may be novel today, and so under Uranus, tomorrow may become stale and pass under the dominion of Saturn. Hence the effects of Uranus and Saturn are antithetical. Those having the Moon configured at birth with Uranus are "born before their time." Ahead of others in thought, they are looked upon as odd, eccentric. Being free from tradition they see and seize opportunities which others pass by. Their originality makes for marked success. In all fields of life they shine, especially in those of commerce, speculation, gambling and sport. Many millionaires have this natal configuration.

*With Neptune*: Being supersensitive souls—the consequence of an exaggerated imagination—they are all too easily stung by an unkind work. These people fight shy of the harsh realities of everyday life and like to escape into a fantastic world of their own creation, of superstition, of memories of the past, of mythology or a world of art, music or dancing. For some it is a world of drugs and opiates. With their overwrought imagination they are easily imposed on. In the world of reality they tend to adopt a distinctive pose or to dress artistically. Being temperamental they are liable to hysteria. When forced out into the open they dither, get worried and flurried. This is a marked characteristic of an afflicted Neptune. The average Neptunian is regarded as somewhat irresponsible.

**With Pluto**: *Th*e most antisocial of the planets, Pluto is the significator of detachment, isolation and extreme loneliness. Those having this configuration at birth are shy when forced to appear amongst others, are quickly bored and take the first opportunity to disappear. They always appear in a state of revolt and are beings apart. Some have to flee from the law. They can stand alone and be unique. Those mingling with society always manage to preserve their independence and detachment. Difficult members of any team, averse to the party system, many distinguish themselves on stage or platform, retaining their aloofness in spite of the applause of the multitude. Sometimes their shyness makes them self-defensively aggressive. This is more noticeable if Pluto is also configured with Mars.

**The Progressions of the Moon**

As a general rule progressions and transits of the Moon to the planets signify the emotional actions of the native, i.e., what he does to others.

On the other hand progressions and transits of the planets to the Moon signify the reactions of the native to the actions taking place in his environment, i.e., what other people or things do to him.

*To the Sun*: For both sexes, but more particularly for the female, the progression of the Moon to a configuration of the natal or progressed Sun presages a union of the sexes, generally but not always in wedlock. In the male geniture it often merely tallies with sexual intercourse. But even so, it underlines an event, however short-lived, that is not without its lasting psychological overtones. Under this progression women tend to homologate their interest in the opposite sex.

*To Mercury*: When the progressed Moon configures the radical or progressed Mercury the native will find himself much occupied, giving talks or lectures, entering into discussions or instructing others. Under this aspect he becomes a teacher. Note that under the aspect of Mercury to the Moon he becomes a pupil.

*To Venus*: When the progressed Moon configures the radical or progressed Venus the native will make love to another. Invitations to weddings or other social gatherings will occur. The opposite aspect, progressed Venus to Moon, will tend to make him or her be wooed by another.

*To Mars*: This aspect finds the native intensely alive, active, dashing from place to place, and working at full stretch. In the impetuosity of his zeal he is apt to be unguarded and outspoken and say things that give offense. In extreme cases he may run up against the law of libel. He will be more belligerent than usual. Under this aspect a statesman might declare war.

*To Jupiter*: This is an aspect which boosts the self-esteem of the native. He may be honoured by those in authority by an invitation to take part in a festivity. For such an occasion the native will endeavour to be on his best behaviour.

***To Saturn***: A series of frustrations occur when the progressed Moon configures the radical or progressed Saturn. It often tallies with a period, often temporary, of cessation of work, enforced idleness and loss of revenue. It synchronises with retirement, resignation or dismissal. A depressing period when nothing seems to thrive.

***To Uranus***: Under this progression the native seeks freshness and is all for change. Shuffling off the old, he makes alterations in his life, changes in his job, removes to a new house or travels. He is moved to do things he has never done before and which are a novelty for him. These novelties break up his old habits.

***To Neptune***: Here the native will thirst for sensation and tend to indulge himself to excess or engage in unseemly conduct leading to his own mortification. The effects will be worse if Neptune is configured with the malefics. Often the native will find himself as a visitor at a hospital, if not an inmate.

***To Pluto***: Under this configuration the native will avail himself of every opportunity to free himself, if only temporarily, from the ties which hold him prisoner. He might, for example, buy a motor [car] to escape from the restrictions of the home. He may take a ready excuse to break up the home life. Sometimes, feeling the restrictions of law or morality, youths may land themselves in serious trouble.

# Mercury

Mercury in the foreground of any map awakens and activates the mental processes of the native. Under this influence he imparts to others what he knows. According to his station in life he may, for example, preach sermons, give lectures, instruct others or write, debate, criticize, discuss or publish.

**Natal Configurations**

***With Venus***: The mind is sweet, tactful and gentle in speech, poetic with a penchant for belles-lettres and the arts, and given to acts of kindness and charity.

***With Mars***: The mind in inclined to competition, such as war and sports or all things mechanical. Exulting in its own strength, it joys in destruction for its own sake and delights in splitting hairs in an argument.

***With Jupiter***: The mind inclines to all things which make for exaltation and betterment, according to the native's point of view, such as theology, statesmanship, consular service, politics, law and university life. The speech is cultured and polished. Should Mars be configured with Jupiter it is inclined to be more gruff, boisterous and militant.

*With Saturn*: Here the mind becomes slower-witted, ponderous, laborious, dubious, skeptical, morose, philosophical or melancholic. Simultaneously configured with Mars and Saturn—the diathesis of disease—the poisoned mind becomes cruel, vindictive, back-biting. There is a tendency towards foul language. It may take a delight in getting others into trouble and rejoices in disciplining them.

*With Uranus*: The mind is inclined to see the novel point of view, is extremely witty, quick in repartee and adroit in saying the unexpected to the delight or chagrin of others.

*With Neptune*: The mind is highly sensitive and imaginative and inclines to art, symbolism and mysticism. Being visual it is often blessed with a photographic memory. The native can excel as a clairvoyant or thought reader.

*With Pluto*: Configured with the coldest and most remote of the planets, the mind is attracted to most things which are austere, forbidding and bizarre. Frequently agnostics, the mind of the native does not function in normal channels. Many, having the mentality of explorers, can live happily in cold, lonely and inaccessible places. This configuration is frequently found in the genitures of those vowed to silence or those who work in secret or dare not voice their thoughts to the public. It is not uncommon in the maps of those who have a speech affliction, especially should Pluto be angular.

### The Progressions of Mercury

The progressions of Mercury appear to have the same effect as its transits and are shown under that heading. The effects of the progressions are, however, longer lasting.

## Venus

Natal and progressed Venus symbolize the "heart" of the native, the love that he feels and gives for another, its action being centrifugal. On the other hand, transiting Venus represents the love which is given by another to the native, its action being centripetal. When in elevation or in the foreground at birth, the native is dominated by his love for others—nothing else matters. It is the motive of his existence. Known as the "venerable" Venus in advanced years, the native may, if in a position to do so, become noted for his philanthropy and charity. In his youth there is something of the Casanova. When in propinquity to one of the inactive places, love is apt to occupy a subordinate place in the life. So placed, marriage is apt to be delayed or altogether denied.

The types of humanity which win the affection of the native may be deduced from the constellation occupied by Venus at birth. For instance, in Aries, the affections may be lavished on those who wield power, the politician or military world. In Sagittarius, clergymen, doctors and the titled. In Aquarius, those interested in out of the way subjects. The constellation [in which Venis is posited] often describes the fetishes of the frustrated.

*Natal Configurations*: Venus is in love with any planet with which it is configured at birth, not excluding malefics.

*With Mars*: Passion matures early in life—the attachment is to the young and vigorous. Not averse to horseplay, the passions are easily inflamed. Hot and tempestuous affairs are many and fraught with risk. If Jupiter comes in too, these affairs can be prolific and extravagant. If configured simultaneously with Saturn, the erotic impulses may become warped or stunted. There may be little feeling for the opposite sex.

*With Jupiter*: Configured alone with Jupiter, it is an auspicious augury for a happy, normal and contented love life. Often the native marries into an affluent family. If Venus is configured with both Jupiter and Saturn, the love instinct takes time to mature. The marriage is often to a near relation, not a stranger. After marriage the native is faithful to the mate for the rest of his days.

*With Saturn*: With this aspect the erotic emotions are slow to evolve, sometimes never. The native feels cold in love. Frankly it is an aspect often found in the horoscopes of confirmed bachelors and spinsters. They may however be attracted to older men.

*With Uranus*: Here the native may well find himself deviating from the normal, this configuration in extreme cases being often found in the maps of homosexuals. They can be normal but are likely to be in search of the fresh, the new, and can in consequence find themselves in endless trouble. Marriage can be a risky venture.

*With Neptune*: With this aspect the native is inclined to be hopelessly romantic in matters of love. In some ways there is an element of the theatre in their affairs. Both Shakespeare and Rudolph Valentino had this conjunction in Taurus.

*With Pluto*: These natives never seem (especially if male) to mature sexually, and the opposite sex in consequence never takes them seriously. When in company with the opposite sex they become embarrassed and act childishly. They are inclined to avoid love. The effects of this configuration resemble those of Venus-Saturn; many never marry. Some even find their release in perversion.

**The Progressions of Venus**

The progressions of Venus appear to have the same effects as those of Venus in transit and will be found under the heading "Transits." The student must however remember that progressions denote incidents, and transits denote accidents. The effects of progressions are more protracted and enduring than those of transits.

# Mars

Unpolished diamonds, rough, uncouth, loudmouthed, clamorous, noisy, wiry, muscular, untidy, prone to swearing and cursing, hot headed, impetuous, brave, daring, reckless, spoiling for a fight, delighting in sport, machinery and mechanics, easily succumbing to temptation, exulting in conflict. These are some of the familiar characteristics of those born with Mars in the foreground. Fundamentally Mars is a "killer"; he destroys for the sheer love of it. The exercise of power gives him immense gratification but there is nothing essentially cruel or vindictive about him.

## Natal Configurations

*With Jupiter*: If Mars is configured with Jupiter, especially in a male geniture, we get those specimens of manhood who are so much admired by the fair sex and schoolboys alike. Because of their sagacity, self-control, sense of fairness and dislike of wanton destruction, they quickly get to the top in the field of sport, in all contests, in the [military] services and also in the field of surgery. They become captains or leaders. They are essentially virile, even in advanced age. They despise all forms of cowardice or brutality to women and children. It can be an aspect of victory.

*With Saturn*: If Mars is configured with Saturn and in the foreground or configured with the luminaries, the male characteristics are apt to be retarded in growth, making the native servile, incapable of manly acts and unpopular with women. To compensate for this feeling they often struggle to control women and children, those whom they consider weaker than themselves. This is one of the most grievous of natal formations as it tends to taint planets they contact with disease, decay and corruption. They will try to control others but what they need is self-control.

*With Uranus*: This is one of the most thrilling and audacious of all configurations. Aspecting the lights it denotes reckless daredevils who, on the spur of the moment, do the most daring things and yet live to tell the tale. As Uranus is the significator of all that is up-to-date, this configuration represents the latest in lethal weapons. Mars and Uranus culminated exactly at Hiroshima when the atomic bomb was dropped. It tends to make military genius.

*With Neptune*: Because of Neptune's imaginative and emotional instability, its configuration with Mars is one of the most dangerous that can occur. No soldier having these planets radically aspecting the lights should be put in a position of power or authority. Symbolizing quantity rather than quality, Neptune so configured could bring about immense carnage or mass slaughter at the whim of the momentarily unbalanced. Famous for his flamboyant military poses, the ex-Kaiser Wilhelm II of Germany, who was held responsible for World War I, was born with Mars and Neptune culminating. It can be an aspect of defeat.

***With Pluto***: Should Mars configure Pluto, the native, if forced to engage in any form of war, will take to the hills as a guerilla or as an "invisible" soldier, but one who takes care, if danger threatens, to leave the way open for his escape.

**The Progressions of Mars**

The interpretation of the progressions follows that of the transiting planet. They will accordingly be found in the transit section. The effects of progressions will however last longer and be deeper.

# Jupiter

Bestowing quality and richness, Jupiter, the greatest of the planets, ennobles the influence of every planet it configures, preserving, healing, protecting, unceasingly. In more senses than one it represents the good. When placed in the foreground natally it generally indicates that the native is born a gentleman, having the benefits of a good parentage and an excellent education. It could be that these advantages are attained through his own efforts in later years. Jupiter, at all times, stands for the best of everything. Hence those who are fortunate enough to be born when it is dominant usually go to the best schools, wear the most stylish clothes, belong to the best clubs, consort with the best people, or enter the best professions, often the church, the law, consular services, the army or medicine. Those whose incomes are derived from the land, real estate, wills, legacies, bequests or from the interest from money held in trust, usually have Jupiter natally configured with Saturn, whilst those who amass a fortune through their own efforts but more especially through speculation, have Jupiter configured with Uranus. For a time show business brings prosperity to those having Jupiter configured with Neptune, but the money is soon dissipated. Its configuration with Pluto savours of ill-gotten prosperity.

**The Progressions of Jupiter**

Jupiter, a slow-moving planet, will not make many aspects by progression during the average life. The general influence of these progressions will be found under the section on transits. The influence will, however, be deeper and longer lasting.

# Saturn

Astrologically, the effects of Saturn are like the appearance of a Flanders landscape immediately after World War I: utterly devastating. The planet represents the long concealed and least presentable facet of our nature, our nothingness which may be in fact our true being, all else being a gaudy facade. It is the grinning spectacle within the comely flesh. A dull leaden weight, devoid of life and movement, it is cold, hard, barren, inactive, without emotion, without sentimentality. As the significator of time (Chronos), it denotes past history, tradition, memory, one's yesterdays and all things that are dead and moribund. Its touch taints all things with the seeds of corruption and decay.

**Progressions of Saturn**

Saturn will rarely make aspects by progression. When it does the effect will be similar to that of the transits of this planet but more prolonged. See the transit section.

# Uranus

Essentially the man before his time, the Uranian will always be found in the vanguard of all advanced movements, discarding the old, the outmoded and the inept for that which is ultra-modern. Being fundamentally a scientist, he typifies the computer age simply because it is the latest advance in progress. Because their outlook, rapid thinking and unexpected actions are new and daring, Uranians in every field of endeavour succeed where others fail. In politics, such people must seem dictators because their fellow workers are too slow-witted to keep pace with them. The best Uranians are the inspired geniuses of humanity. Their rapidity of thought and quick action give them success in sport, in speculation and in all financial dealings. When the Uranian turns to crime, only another Uranian can catch him. Having vision and the capacity for rapid thinking and for making snap decisions in times of crisis they may take important office. As soon as it is over they may be dropped again.

**Progressions of Uranus**

Uranus will not normally make progressions except to planets with which it is in orb at birth.

# Neptune

It is important to distinguish between the excitement produced by Uranus and that produced by Neptune. The former is mental, the latter emotional. The excitement of going on a holiday or of getting a new car is Uranian, whilst that occasioned by repeated curtain calls is Neptune. When stimulated, Neptune is prone to cause emotional excitement so that, completely flurried, the native does not know whether he is coming or going. Its greatest manifestations will be witnessed at cup finals and the like when the mighty surge of excitement, sweeping the crowd irresistibly on, can lead to catastrophe. The apprehension occasioned by the arrival of bad news can become so exaggerated by the imagination that the native trembles and is in a blue funk.

Whilst Saturn is responsible for the educational or social sense of inferiority, Neptune is the cause of an indefinable sense of inadequacy that makes him shirk responsibility of all kinds and gives the wish to escape into a secluded leisurely world of congeniality which, absorbing his whole interest, is shut against all intruders from the actual world of everyday life. In this sequestered world of one's dreams, one can indulge one's hobbies to one's heart's content. This is the world of art, music, and literature, of fiction and science.

**Natal Configurations of Neptune**

*With Sun*: Dreams may become true as with the case of Edison and Marconi.

*With Moon*: The imaginative, sensitive side of this aspect may make a popular novelist of genius like Charles Dickens.

*With Mercury*: The native may lose himself to this world in lengthy experiments with mathematical equations, chemical formulae or positional astronomy.

*With Venus*: Poetry and belles-lettres are the magnet, as with Shakespeare.

**Progressions of Neptune**

Neptune will not form progressions except by the closing of a natal aspect.

# Pluto

The appearance conferred by Pluto when in the immediate foreground at birth is always such as to arrest attention because it stands out from the crowd. Amongst men, full, shaggy beards are frequent. The drooping eyelids and the distant and disdainful glance at one down the nose of those who have a prominent Pluto in the constellation of Cancer reminds one of the dromedary. Pluto is a solitary worker, a bad mixer, the odd man out, the eternal lone wolf. Sooner or later he breaks clear from this home, putting behind him all it represents in respectability, tradition and orthodoxy, for at heart he is the eternal rebel. Shyness, diffidence, remoteness, austerity, cynicism and a sardonic smile are characteristic of this planet.

# Transits

The transits of the rapidly moving Sun and Moon will only be of importance when they occur in the immediate foreground of the chart or if they are configured with other planets. The effect of these will be similar but much weaker than those of the progressions which have already been given in another section.

**The Sun on an Angle of Return Maps**

The appearance of the Sun on an angle attracts attention to the native. He becomes self-reliant and unsure of himself. He may take the chair or act in some similar capacity. The understanding will be clear-sighted, he will be at his best. For healers, this is a good position.

### The Moon on an Angle

The usual effect of this position is that another, emotionally inclined, may seek the company of the native. In political maps the Moon, representing the public, is favourable for statesmen seeking election.

## Mercury

### Mercury in the Foreground of a Return Map

The native often finds himself a passenger by land, sea or air. He may receive an important communication.

### The Transits of Mercury

It must be remembered that these transits are so rapid that they can pass without effect. They will have some effect when Mercury is prominent by being in the foreground. When this aspect appears as a progression it will be more effective.

*To the Moon*: This transit may find the native visiting libraries or lectures in pursuit of knowledge. The progression will be of longer duration and more powerful.

*To Mercury*: When stationary and in the foreground, information, a letter, book, etc., may be received which will affect his work.

*To Venus*: An affectionate letter may arrive under this transit or progression. If configured simultaneously with the malefics there will be disappointment.

*To Mars*: This transit or progression can lead to the use of force or violence. It sometimes finds the native engaged in sport or manual work.

*To Jupiter*: An excellent transit for seeking promotion and interviewing the manager. Good for addressing meetings. But note whether Mercury is free from afflictions.

*To Saturn*: Even though they may be beneficial these transits are never pleasant and may be humiliating. All transits to Saturn make one uncomfortable.

### Transits to the outer planets

All such transits to the outer planets affect the same age group and are not important personally unless Mercury is prominent and the transit is in the foreground.

*To Uranus*: Often occurs during removal to a new place. Surprises in the course of travel.

*To Neptune*: In the course of travel the native may attend a concert or visit the opera.

*To Pluto*: In some cases under this transit the native has been found to be on the run, trying to escape his obligations.

# Venus

## Natal Venus on an Angle of Return Maps

When natal Venus appears in the immediate foreground of any sidereal chart the affections of the native are liable to be stirred into action. The effect will be greater if Venus is simultaneously transited by another planet.

## Transiting Venus on an Angle

When transiting Venus comes into the foreground it generally indicates a pleasant time. It often happens that another person sees the native for the first time or after a long separation and is charmed and expresses good will and affection. The native becomes the recipient of favours, invitations and tokens of esteem. How he reacts to these depends on the nature of simultaneous transits.

## The Transits of Venus

*To the Sun*: Unless Venus is prominent in some way this transit by a rapidly moving planet may pass unnoticed. If slow in motion the native may be honoured in some way be being invited to a party at which he will look his best.

*To the Moon*: Under such a transit the native may pay special attention to his wardrobe. Should Venus be with Uranus he may adopt new modes of attire. If a male he will at this time be popular with women.

*To Mercury*: Not an important transit. It can harmonize the mind, writing done at this time will be felicitous in expression.

*To Venus*: A rapid transit which may have no effect. But love at first sight has happened under this transit. With progressions this aspect can only happen when Venus, turning retrograde, returns to its radical longitude.

*To Mars*: When prominent, Venus transiting Mars causes another person to be atracted to the native who may be mutually attracted. There have been hasty marriages under this transit.

*To Jupiter*: Under this transit the native usually becomes the recipient of tokens of esteem and affection from admirers.

*To Saturn*: Should Venus be prominent at the time, attempts by another to contact the native may be rejected. There may even be disgust at the approach.

*To Uranus*: Romance meets the native when on an adventure.

*To Neptune*: Pleasure comes to the native when Venus transits Neptune. He usually fmds it in his hobbies and pastimes. He may receive gifts useful for these hobbies.

*To Pluto*: Under unusual circumstances a stranger seeks the companionship of the native.

# Mars

### Natal Mars on an Angle of a Return Maps

When radical Mars appears on an angle in return maps the native is prepared to attack, annoy, tease, be generally aggressive to others and even to use force.

### Transiting Mars on an Angle

When transiting Mars appears in the foreground it presages some physical hurt, injury, fever or indisposition the severity of which depends on the speed of Mars at the time and on its aspects. The common cold often appears under this aspect. Transits to the outer planets are only important when occurring in the immediate foreground.

*To the Moon*: The native will be irascible and his temper anything but docile. Sometimes there is a visit to the dentist or surgeon. Should Mars and Saturn together transit the Moon in the foreground the native is in danger of violence at the hands of others.

*To Mercury*: Criticism of the native's ideas may cause him to react vigorously in their defense. Should Mars and Jupiter together transit Mercury the native will triumph. Should Mars and Saturn transit Mercury the native will find that his ideas and theories of any kind are demolished.

*To Venus*: When the hot and impetuous Mars transits radical Venus, the love nature of the native becomes inflamed and he may fmd himself falling passionately in love. Should transiting Jupiter be also configured with Mars his overtures to another meet with success. Should Saturn be with Mars he will fmd himself scorned and snubbed. For the engaged or married this dual transit of the malefics is an ill omen.

*To Jupiter*: The native usually discovers he has spent more money than he can afford when Mars transits Jupiter. There is some danger of fife destroying property. If Saturn joins in, there is a danger of theft. With Uranus of losses on the stock exchange or through gambling.

*To Saturn*: The most ugly of all transits is that of Mars over radical Saturn. Now the native can feel hatred. He may become unpopular and may be maligned and made to feed unwanted. He may be forced to resign from a position. He may have to submit to discipline.

***To Uranus***: Mars in transit over Uranus often causes unpleasant events occurring quite unexpectedly. Sometimes in the course of travel it is an accident formation.

***To Neptune***: This transit can cause panic and agitation from which he does not recover soon. In some way he may be driven into a corner. It is a transit of defeat.

***To Pluto***: A "shock" transit which may cause a nervous condition. In extreme cases the native may be under suspicion of an offence.

# Jupiter

## Natal Jupiter on an Angle of a Return Map

Occurring frequently it generally finds the native at his best, provided that it is not afflicted. It is an excellent opportunity to interview superiors to seek promotion. He is then likely to cause the best of impressions because he feels at his best.

## Transiting Jupiter on an Angle

This is the best of all possible transits even though it may last but a day. It gives rise to such emotions as joy, elation and happiness. Even when under bad directions, should this transit occur on the day of an election the native will win. This transit often brings with it prizes and money rewards. We should, however, check on the other aspects to Jupiter; but these will rarely keep Jupiter in check.

## The Transits of Jupiter

***To the Sun***: Although nothing of significance appears to happen when Jupiter transits radical or progressed Sun, it is at this time that the seeds of enduring prosperity are sown. Seemingly insignificant jobs undertaken under such a transit may at a later time blossom into success. In accordance with his bent, it is at this time that the native may join a religious or occult society which may be even at a later time of worldly benefit to him.

***To the Moon***: This is an excellent transit in every way. The health of the native will improve, he will be optimistic, popular and fortunate.

***To Mercury***: Under this transit the way is paved for the native to carry out his long cherished schemes regarding the office. It is a good time for making speeches. His mental work will flourish. As a boy he will shine at school.

***To Venus***: The course of true love runs smoothly when Jupiter transits radical Venus. A very happy time when things run well.

***To Mars:*** The transit of Jupiter over Mars finds the native full of energy, physically fit and indulging successfully in sport, motoring, racing or in any activity, even in his garden. For the professional soldier on active service it is excellent.

*To Saturn*: Any transit to radical Saturn always carries with it the stigma of embarrassment and even humiliation. That of Jupiter is no exception. Under it the prodigal son returns, the exile is recalled, another pays his debts; all is forgiven.

*To Uranus*: The native is moved to do something completely different and excitingly novel when Jupiter transits the radical Uranus, such as travel to out of the way places, to undertake a lecture tour or in general to try many things which prove entertaining and exciting

*To Neptune*: The native will generally get more fun out of his hobbies, indulging them in a big way when Jupiter transits radical Neptune. He will probably spend more money on them than he can afford. He may, for instance, join in amateur theatricals, take up golf or learn the twist.

*To Pluto*: This transit brings relief to the hard-pressed. In one case a blackmailer was arrested.

# Saturn

## Natal Saturn on an Angle of a Return Map

The occasions are most unpleasant when the natal Saturn appears in the immediate foreground of return maps. The effect is naturally increased if it simultaneously suffers the transit of a malefic. On such an occasion one feels alone, empty, insufficient, inadequate, neglected, miserable, uncared for and unloving, suffering from chronic ailments.

Some of the worst periods are when the angles progress to configurations of the radical or progressed Saturn. They usually mark periods of enforced idleness, poverty, hardship and even hunger and want. Such a progression, particularly that of the progressed Ascendant, usually tallies with illness. In advanced age this is a serious configuration.

## Transiting Saturn on the Angles

This is the worst of omens for success. Often it denotes failure in all things. It denotes the ill will—even hatred—of others, which inhibits success at this time. It is an aspect of unpopularity. It is the cause of endless waiting, delays, inferior quality and disappointments.

## The Transits of Saturn

*To the Sun*: If the native is wise he would be advised to hibernate and go slow when this transit is acting. Anything new that he undertakes is not likely to be a success. It is a time for holding on and not for new undertakings. Under such a transit Hitler began the war. Generally under this transit the malice of the world seems turned against the native and stumbling blocks appear in his path. It is a precarious time and he should be cautious. Business will be poor and progress retarded.

*To the Moon*: Under this transit not a few of the mighty fall from power. The failure of their schemes and growing opposition deflates their self-esteem and they tend to sink into a state of melancholy and inactivity. These are extreme cases such as happened with Napoleon after the retreat from Moscow and with Hitler in the bunker in Berlin. For the ordinary individual, distasteful changes cause him to be dispirited and depressed; in extreme cases he becomes physically ill.

*To Mercury*: Under this transit criticism of his beliefs and theories embitters the native. Doubts assailing the mind, he feels his security in jeopardy. Unpleasant questions are disturbing and he may have to undertake uncongenial work, often in different surroundings.

*To Venus*: Under the impact of Saturn's transit, friends neglect the native, his sweetheart deserts him for another. His wardrobe falls into neglect. Consorting with bad companions he may visit doubtful resorts.

*To Mars*: When Saturn transits natal Mars, the native, finding himself thwarted and pushed around, is apt to try and take it out on the weaker, such as wife and children and to act the bully. Hurting out of viciousness in battle or in sport, he meets with ill-success. Should Venus be with Saturn there may be sadistic tendencies.

*To Saturn*: Janus-like, the transit of Saturn to its own natal place often closes one door and opens another. Through no fault of his own he may be dismissed and find himself unemployed. It sometimes happens that he finds another job at once. It is a worrying and anxious time for the native, the more so if he tries to shoulder additional responsibilities.

**To the Outer Planets**

These will affect millions of the same age group and generally do not concern individuals.

# Uranus

### Natal Uranus on an Angle of a Return Map

Other things being equal the coming of radical Uranus to the foreground is exhilarating. Stretching his legs the native sets off in search of fresh fields and new pastures. Getting away from routine, it affords an opportunity to do something different and perhaps get a thrill or shock. The native will search for the new.

## Transiting Uranus on an Angle

The unexpected and often the exciting happens when Uranus transits the immediate foreground of a return map. Should Uranus be also configured with the benefics he will meet strangers under unusual circumstances and have an interesting and exciting time. If configured with the malefics such meetings can be anything but fortunate. The possibility of accidents cannot be excluded. In short, the new intrudes on the native.

## The Transit of Uranus to the Planets

*To the Sun*: If it is not spoiled by the simultaneous transit of the malefics this transit may prove to be the most exciting and exhilarating of the life. Under it the native may be transferred to a new job, may even make a discovery or may decide to break with routine and tradition and to do something entirely different. There can be an impulse to go on an extensive tour, but from this the native will return to his former habits.

*To the Moon*: This transit over the Moon and especially the progressed Moon often finds the native on the move the whole time in search of thrills. The motorist will seek thrill in speed to the terror of others. He may change his residence, often more than once. It is a period of adventure.

*To Mercury*: When not afflicted this is one of the most exciting transits that can occur. Following a period of mental doldrums a sudden flash of inspiration illuminates the mind followed by a period of creativity. Under it the native may come to a study of astrology or of similar subjects. Many scientific discoveries are due to it.

*To Venus*: A whirlwind romance often occurs under this transit. Under its influence the native may fall for a complete stranger, get married in a hurry and just as quickly get separated again. It is the most glamorous of all transits and the most hectic.

*To Mars*: The transit of Uranus over radical Mars finds the native impulsively taking hair-raising risks that he would be too scared to do at any other time such as exceeding the speed limit, cutting in with his automobile, parachuting and the like. Under this transit some have succeeded as hypnotists. Through sheer daring and good timing many soldiers have been decorated, and many surgeons have performed successfully tricky operations.

*To Jupiter*: The transit of Uranus over radical Jupiter can make or break the native financially. On the morrow he may find himself a millionaire or a ruined man. All depends on accompanying aspects. If these are benefics, it indicates sudden wealth by speculation or gambling; if malefics, sudden losses by the same means.

*To Saturn*: Although the transit of Uranus to natal Saturn can be very serious it must be remembered that it affects all of the same age group. To be personal this transit must fall in the immediate foreground. Even then it may be due to national calamity. In extreme cases dormant hate can become accentuated, leading the native to commit crime.

Transits to the outer planets affect all of the same age group and need not be considered individually.

# Neptune

### Natal Neptune on an Angle of a Return Map

Provided that it is not afflicted by transiting malefics, transiting Neptune makes the native feel like taking "French leave" to escape from his responsibilities and to bury himself in his pet distractions. At this time he may succumb to his favourite temptation.

### Transiting Neptune on an Angle

This transit will usually find the native in an intense, if somewhat suppressed, state of emotional excitement, a state of worry and flurry. Under such transits school boys have to report to the headmaster, the aching to the dentist, the afflicted to the surgeon. States of anaesthesia are characteristic of Neptune. There is a possibility of being victimized or robbed, even of becoming inebriated. Neptune too, has a connection with seduction. On the positive side the native may well make a positive achievement in the realm of art.

### Transits of Neptune to the Planets

*To the Sun*: The native tends to feel all sorts of imaginary terrors when Neptune transits the Sun. He may develop an inferiority complex and feel scorned and neglected. In this state of heightened imagination he suffers from constant apprehension. Although nothing serious may happen it is a period that he would like to forget.

*To the Moon*: Under this rare transit the native discovers to his dismay that those nearest and dearest to him have been deceiving him perhaps for a long time. To the married such a discovery may break up married life. The effects may put him in a state of nervous excitement lasting some time.

*To Mercury*: The mind finds itself indulging in illusion, make-believe, fiction, drama, music. In some way a sense of reality is lost.

*To Venus*: Full of romance, make-believe and otherworldliness, the native is apt to fall for the impossible and be accordingly deceived. He tends to become an easy victim for exploiters. A woman may easily fall for an unsuitable partner. Music and dancing may stimulate the mind and cause false attachments.

***To Mars***: A serious transit as uncontrolled emotion, such as caused by crowd activities, a sudden sense of power as in war, the helplessness of others, may tempt the native to acts of cruelty which are otherwise not in his nature.

***To Jupiter***: The transit of Neptune over Jupiter signifies bogus wealth and fictitious prosperity, money gained by mortgages and loans, pledging one's possessions in a pawn shop, or in these modern days, in a hire-purchase scheme.

***To Saturn***: In extreme cases this transit may cause dirty linen to be washed in public. If in the foreground it can be serious, the native being in some way disgraced and in extreme cases ruined.

***To Uranus and Pluto***: Such transits need not be considered personally as they affect millions of the same age group.

## Pluto

### Natal Pluto on an Angle of a Return Map

Unless it simultaneously suffers transits, the effects of the appearance of natal Pluto in the immediate foreground may pass unnoticed.

### Transiting Pluto on an Angle

When transiting Pluto is in the immediate foreground it gives the native a shock and indeed often a very nasty jolt. This fact makes Pluto the most useful of all planets for rectification. It acts without warning and its effects can be very intense but often more psychological than physical. It occasions such nerve-shattering and unexpected events as the sudden death of the parents, police raids, being questioned by the police, being robbed and even beaten up. The underlying influence makes one want to take to one's heels and get clear. Pluto in transit has exposed secrets in the cupboard. We can be caught red-handed. The effects are far more unexpected than those of Uranus and more nerve-shattering.

Transiting Pluto on an angle often represents the end of the beginning or the beginning of the end as it seems to usher in definite stages of the life of the native or of a country.

### The Transits of Puto

***To the Sun***: To the aged this is the saddest transit that can occur. Under such a transit they may find that they are unwanted, especially by the young. They feel desolate and alone. Even the young under this transit can feel isolated. When configured with the malefics, especially Mars, it is a violent combination causing family feuds, the severing of ties, separation and divorce. In mundane astrology it is one of the most pregnant causes of war.

**To *the Moon*:** Occurring only once, if ever, in the lifetime, this transit is of considerable importance, presaging a revolutionary change in one's menage. Under its impact circumstances may induce one to pull up one's roots and emigrate. Influenced by propaganda youths may join revolutionary bodies seeking liberty and thereby get themselves into trouble.

**To *Mercury*:** For some odd reason whilst this transit is on, the mind refuses to pay attention to what is being said with bad effects on study. The mind may wander away from the trodden path to explore untrodden ways in knowledge. There may at this period be a nervous affliction.

**To *Venus*:** It has been difficult to find case histories to study this transit. Getting little satisfaction from normal congress the native may seek gratification in eccentricity.

**To *Mars*:** Fortunately this transit can occur only once in the life and may not occur at all. It is a violent transit which forces the native to show hostility to someone, often against his inclinations. The criminally inclined operating as lone hands have committed serious violent crime under this influence.

**To *Jupiter*:** According to its co-lateral configurations, money may be gained or lost, often illegally, in extreme cases through war, loot, or stolen property.

**To *Saturn*:** The effects of this transit are somewhat similar to the transit of Neptune, although the psychology is different. It is a transit which will humble and mortify the native.

### Transits to the Outer Planets

Such transits are of a general effect and will not be considered individually.

## Hints on the Interpretation of Solunars

Consider first and foremost planets in conjunction with an angle, allowing an orb of up to some six degrees.

Consider planets which are in conjunction or opposition with these angular planets and those which are in square aspect. These will modify judgment.

Planets which are in square to the M.C. or the Ascendant are also important.

Planets in these positions form the basis of any interpretation of solunars.

Planets widely distant from the angles can give a negative clue in that for the period of the return map they are inactive.

With angular planets, distinguish between natal and transiting planets in accordance with the interpretation given in this chapter. Generally, transiting planets bring an outside influence into the life and natal planets represent our personal reaction to circumstances.

In considering the interpretations given, seek to find the underlying general meaning of a combination or transit. It is obviously impossible to give all possible manifestations.

In solunars we have not found that house positions with their traditional interpretations are of importance.

It has been found that when both a natal planet and the same transiting planet are prominent by angular position the event is likely to be of greater importance.

The interpretation of solunars is both an art and a science.

## The Novien

In the pages of *American Astrology*, overwhelming evidence has been published demonstrating that the great nations of antiquity, such as Egypt, Babylon, Assyria, the Arabs, the Jews, and the Hindus, used zodiacal constellations which commenced with Taurus and ended with Aries; or with the surrogate for Aries as that constellation is altogether missing from the Babylonian version of the zodiac. Unlike the Greco-Roman constellations of unequal lengths, the figures of which grace our modern star atlases, the zodiacal constellations of remote antiquity were rigidly thirty degrees in extent. They commenced with the asterism of the Pleiades; its fiducial or marking star was Aldebaran, The Bull's Eye, permanently fixed in Taurus 15° 00′ 00″, the mathematical center of the constellation.

We must always remember that the fundamental blunder of the Greeks, otherwise the most intelligent of people, was in their unshakable conviction that the equinoctial points, which always rise due east and set due west, were the only fixed points in the firmament, and which they made the fiducial of their tropical zodiacs, for they had many. The classical zodiac, that is the one in use among the Greeks and the Romans at the time of Christ, commenced with 0 Aries, but with the vernal equinoctial point fixed not in 0 Aries but in 8 Aries 00. This was the zodiac of Manilius, Firmicus, the Pseudo-Manetho, and the majority of the classical writers on, and according to Professor Otto Neugebauer, it persisted right into the Middle Ages *(Greek Horoscopes,* The American Philosophical Society, Philadelphia 1959, p. 12 c.) The longitudes of the planets are shown in the Denderah zodiacs in terms of this version of the tropical zodiac; a tropical zodiac being one in which the vernal point is permanently fixed in a specific degree of the ecliptic. Hipparchus' version of the tropical zodiac with the vernal point fixed in 0 Aries did not become the vogue until the time of Proclus some 400 years later.

When about 129 B.C. Hipparchus discovered the phenomena of precession, he and all the Greek astronomers with him, were fully convinced that it was the fixed stars that precessed, never moved—never, never—the equinoctial points. It was only in the medieval period that Leonardo Da Vinci, Copernicus, and Galileo, in unearthing the Greek blunder, assassinated the tropical zodiac at the foot of the Hennes of Hipparchus, [because it was their ambition and desire that caused the tropical zodiac] to usurp the place of the true zodiac. Unfortunately, no tropical astrologers were present to witness the Fell Deed, and so to this day, under the shadow of the Basilica of St. Peter's, the tropical cadavers lie a' moulding, unknelled, unconfined, but alas, not unknown.

One wonders how many tropical astrologers fully realize that the tropical versions of the zodiac were all conceived and born in error? No amount of sophistry, theo or otherwise, can metamorphose a blatant blunder into a truism—a statement that our university Dons will immediately appreciate.

If astrologers really understood the genesis of the tropical zodiacs and all their implication, they would drop them immediately as they would a viper. Instead, they prefer, ostrich-like, to bury their heads in the sands of their leaders—often as stupid as themselves—to guide them. Yes, we have made immense progress since the days of Egypt and Babylon—in stupidity.

All historical evidence incontestably establishes that the Hindu zodiac of the constellations originally commenced with the *nakshatra krittika,* which was that of the Pleiades and ended with that of *rohini,* the *yogatara* of which is a small star in the constellation Aries. Now the Hindu zodiac commences with *aswini* in 0 Aries and ends with *ravati* (Zeta Piscium), a small star in the constellation Pisces. Why? Even the most learned Hindu pundits have failed to answer this vitally important question. In an article by Professor B.V. Raman entitled *The Paranatellonta of Aswini,* it was demonstrated that the Hindu zodiac of the classical period was *sayana* or tropical! Also the Hindu astrologers of yore—the beloved *maharishis*—wrote and taught tropical astrology. At least two of the writers of the famous *siddhantas,* the standard text books of Hindu astrology, were of western nationality and origin!

When Hindu astrologers were questioned as to why their zodiac was altered from 0 Taurus to 0 Aries they either evaded the question or remained silent. Like our western brethren, being occult but not historically-minded, and having no records, they simply do not know! But to the historically-minded student not infected with chauvinism, it is patently obvious what happened, although not generally admitted by modern denizens of *aryavarta.* When in 326 B.C. at the battle of Hydaspes, Alexander the Great conquered the Punjab, Greece became the master of India and Greeks infiltrated the land. At some time between that date and the epoch of *aryavata* (A.D. 499), the Hindu zodiac was Hellenized, that is to say it was converted into a *sayana* or tropical zodiac, and made to commence with 0 Aries, the vernal point being fixed in 8 Aries according to System B, or in 0 Aries according to the system of Hipparchus, recently in.

But in the course of time, when the occupying powers quit India, that benighted country found itself saddled with a zodiac beginning with Aries which was neither tropical nor sidereal. It is going to take the academically-minded Professor B.V. Raman and his team of intelligent workers all of their time to restore in all its splendour the original zodiac of the *maharishis* of India, which commenced with Taurus. Having achieved this noble work to fmally obliterate Greek influence, they, in their turn, will be numbered among the greatest *maharishis* of all time. In this stupendous task, the astrological world will depend on them not to quail.

Associated in Indian literature with the *rashi* or birth chart is the *navamsa* chart. The latter is obtained by multiplying the sidereal longitude of the Sun, Moon and planets by nine, and ejecting from the product 360 degrees (if included therein) and in all multiples thereof. From the beginning the present writer looked upon such microzodiacs as schematicism pure and simple, and would therefore have nothing to do with it. Moreover, the position of the luminaries and planets in the *navamsas* seem to bear little or no connection with the actual disposition and environment of the native, and failed to reveal, as claimed in the *nadi* literature, the date of birth of the marriage partner. Since 1958, lunar tables are so accurate that it is now possible, notwithstanding the Moon's erratic daily motion, to obtain the Moon's longitude with commendable accuracy to fractions of seconds of arc, and since 1921, all hospital-entered births are recorded here in the U.S.A. to the nearest minute. There is very little excuse in not having the Moon's sidereal longitude as accurate as that of the Sun.

In view of this, the present writer, notwithstanding his prejudice, was moved to have another look at the *navamsa,* especially at the *vimshottari dasa* system, fundamentally based on the same idea, and which depended entirely on the sidereal longitude of the natal Moon worked out so surprisingly accurate for him—even to the minutest detail. He invited Garth Allen's opinion. Almost nonchalantly, Garth replied that if the *navamsas* were to have any validity at all, they must be reckoned from 0 Taurus in lieu of 0 Aries as is the present custom. Without realizing it, in this casual statement, Garth had pressed the magic button that revealed the mystic cavern of the true interpretation of all astrological figures. The astute reader will soon discover the *navamsa* of the Moon thus calculated not only intimately describes one's innermost disposition and the type of environment one was brought up in, but the 2nd or 3rd *navamsa* of the Moon, if not in the first case, for the ladies; and the Sun in the case of the men often indicates the birthday of the husband or the wife, according to the *linganioni* system of selecting one's matrimonial partner. In the matter of intimacies and antipathies, the *navamsa* quite frequently show a planetary relationship not often obvious from an examination of birth charts.

Philogistically, it would appear that the *ayanamsas* had their origin in ancient Egypt, for the Egyptian phonetics for the new moon, *psd* (peshed) and for the number nine were identical! In view of the Sanskrit *navamsa* from time to time, various other names such as the Greek *ennead* and the Latin *nonal* have been adopted by English writers. But these words merely mean the numeral nine. Unless a better one is suggested, it is proposed to use the Latin *novien* which means "nine times," which is more descriptive.

It must not be supposed as our Hindu brethren would have us believe that the novien chart is a secondary geniture. It is nothing of the sort. It is just an aspectarian-vernier. It permits the user to measure micro-aspects that may not be otherwise apparent, especially to the Moon. In the novien chart, the novienic longitude of the Moon is made the cusp of the first house; the remaining eleven houses being calculated on the principle of equal house division, always remembering that here we are dealing with micro-ecliptical mutual configurations, and not with the mundane sphere. Remember that an orb of merely one degree in the birth chart is equivalent to an orb of nine degrees in the novien, so it is not difficult to see how sensitive and critical the novien can be. It would seem the antiquated Egyptians had solved "in minutes" this problem of symbolics some 6,000 years before Messrs. Franklin and Carter had "progressed" to that idea.

But to put the noviens to a practical test: in *The Astrologer's Quarterly* (Vol. 42, No.2) under the caption "Local Zodiacal Influences," Dennis Elwell gives the details of the nativity of "a man for whom sadism and murder became a philosophy of life." He was born in Glasgow, January 2, 1938, at 12:40 p.m., presumably G.M.T. No details as to his name, crime nor dates of his victims were given. In an October 1968 issue of *Esquire,* the author, Kenneth Tynan, gives the name of this man and his mistress as Ian Brady and Myra Hindley, stating his victims were a youth of seventeen and two children of 12 and 10 years old. We are also informed that as a boy this man cut up live cats with a flick knife.

It would appear that the case and trial occurred in 1966, when the writer was sequestered in far-flung Arizona, and learned absolutely nothing of it; and alas, none of his astrological associates in England took the trouble to enlighten him! The case is one of those that occur, if ever, once in the lifetime of the really zealous research student, and it is of the utmost importance as a clinical case where requisite data is available, because in this case the native was born in Scotland where birth times are recorded and available to the public. More important, still, the birth dates and times of his victims and the times of their deaths may also be obtained. For the record, these could enable the astute astrologer to determine precisely the nature of the directions, transits and quotidians at the time of death; but of even greater importance to the astrological world, the fatal planetary interchange that existed between the killer and his hapless victims.

Dennis Elwell rightly contends that "on the face of [it,] this chart (tropical version of his nativity) is no worse than many others, and I venture to say that on the basis of tradition, no astrologer would have guessed at the dark impulses geminating therein." Then comparing this chart with that of Peter Kuerten, he attempts to explain away the man's sadistic impulses to common degree areas [and the line] much in the manner of Maurice Weymiss. But the present writer has been informed that such degree areas when put to rigorous statistical tests fail to produce ratios of any significance. Chart No. 1 is the sidereal version of the native's geniture which is not unusual except for the angularity of the Moon in Sagittarius, which is common to the natal charts of Kuetten and Eichmann. But Chart No. 2 is the corresponding novienic figure, and as the reader can see for himself, it is intensely radix.

The first thing that rivets the attention is that the Ascendant of the novien, which tallies with that of the Moon's novienic longitude, is in Pisces, and statistics have established that more active sadomasochists have the Moon in Pisces than in any other sign. Medieval woodcuts depict Pisces by showing a school boy being pinned down to the punishment block by two junior school teachers while his naked buttock is being soundly birched by the headmaster. The Feast of the Lupercal was celebrated in ancient Rome about February 15 (Sun in Pisces) when naked youths armed with whips would scour the streets and whip any young women or girls found.

Actually, Pisces, now presumed to be ruled by Neptune, is the antithesis of Virgo, ruled by Mercury, God of Flight. While Virgo natives delight to see their offspring at an early age spread their pinions and take to flight, natives of Pisces on the other hand dread to see their children grow up and leave them, and as the tails of the two fish are tied together, symbolizing the umbilical cord that unites the foctus to the mother, so they endeavour to keep their children, their pets, and their treasures chained to them forever. When their children or pets are thus deprived of their freedom, Piscean mothers relish chastising them and by such means enforcing their will.

Sadism is a symptom that the native is undersexed. In such cases the Sun, seat of the vital urge, will be found in strong configuration with Saturn. To work himself into the required state of potency, he must feel power flowing through his being, and usually can only feel that power when he lashes away at some other unfortunate who cannot escape. The more they can hear another yell for mercy, the more potent they feel. That is why the Egyptian Min, the ithyphallic god of potency, is seen on monuments always armed with a flagellum. In this novienic chart, natal Sun in Sagittarius was in conjunction with the triple conjunction of Pluto, Saturn and Uranus. So the native was forced to perform the most fiendish acts of

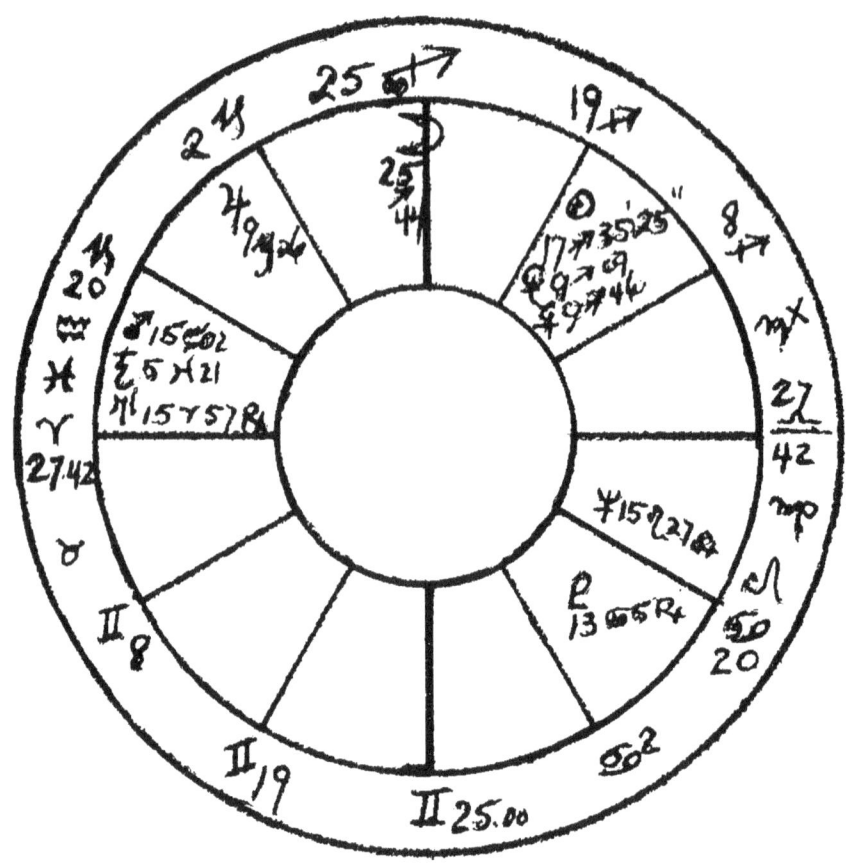

*Chart No. 1, Ian Brady*
*January 2, 1938, 2:40 p.m. GMT, Glasgow*

cruelty to awaken sufficient sexual drive to himself. Perhaps he would be content like celibates to remain permanently in this sexually apathetic state were it not for the opposition of Mars in the boyish Gemini to the natal Sun. In contradiction to the influence of natal Saturn to natal Sun, mutual configurations between the Sun and Mars make one oversexed to a high degree, especially the ladies, and in consequence, their domestic lives are in a frantic state of turmoil. It is these contradictory configurations that made the native the sadist he was.

It is not good looks nor the liberal use of cosmetics that makes for sexual attraction, nor any of the social graces; but a few brisk rubs of the lodestone of Mars. It is Mars' magnetic

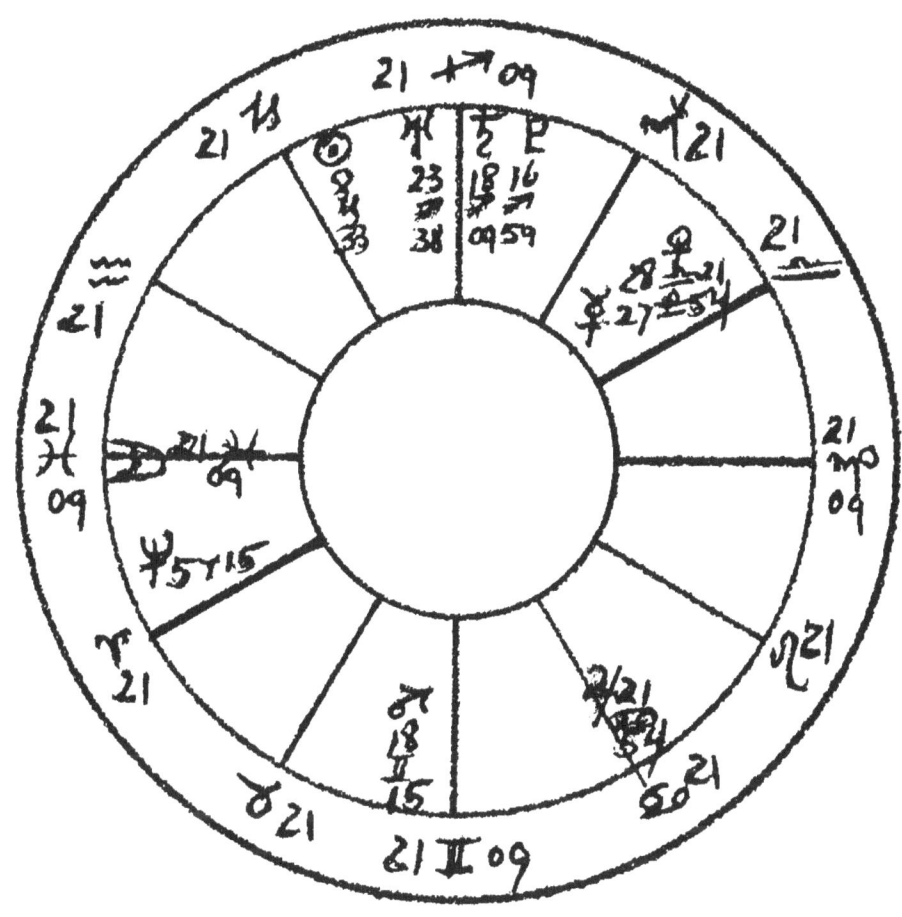

*Chart No. 2, Ian Brady*
*Novienic Equivalent*

power that draws the sexes together and in this respect, we must never forget, as taught by the classic astrologers, that Mars is considered an effeminate planet and symbolizes the place where one gets hurt, however much mythologically considered he is portrayed as the God of War. Astrologically, Mars plays an entirely different role, which one is only too often apt to forget. For instance, should the Sun in one chart be in opposition to Mars in a chart of the opposite sex, then that Sun, and not the Mars person, may use "tooth and claws" to get at the body of the Mars person, often causing the latter considerable physical discomposure if not bodily hurt, which masochists delight in as the pain stimulates their own latent erotic urges. Even the Moon person who has that luminary in conjunction or in opposition with another's Mars will find some fault with that Mars person, as to otherwise make passes at them, lose their temper and strike at them. God help children whose Mars is configured with the Moon in the horoscopes of either of their parents or their teacher.

It is submitted that the novienic Moon in Pisces square aspect to the natal Sun, and to the novienic Pluto, Saturn and Uranus in Sagittarius, and to the novien Mars in Gemini, adequately and perfectly portrays the stated character and disposition of the native.

# The Novienic Table

| | | | *Degrees* | | | | |
|---|---|---|---|---|---|---|---|
| *Taurus* | | *Gemini* | | *Cancer* | | *Leo* | |
| *Virgo* | | *Libra* | | *Scorpio* | | *Sagittarius* | |
| *Capricorn* | | *Aquarus* | | *Pisces* | | *Aries* | |
| 0 = | 0 | 0 = | 0 | 0 = | 0 | 0 = | 0 |
| 1 | 9 | 1 | 9 | 1 | 9 | 1 | 9 |
| 2 | 18 | 2 | 18 | 2 | 18 | 2 | 18 |
| 3 | 27 | 3 | 27 | 3 | 27 | 3 | 27 |
| 4 | 6 | 4 | 6 | 4 | 6 | 4 | 6 |
| 5 | 15 | 5 | 15 | 5 | 15 | 5 | 15 |
| 6 | 24 | 6 | 24 | 6 | 24 | 6 | 24 |
| 7 | 3 | 7 | 3 | 7 | 3 | 7 | 3 |
| 8 | 12 | 8 | 12 | 8 | 12 | 8 | 12 |
| 9 | 21 | 9 | 21 | 9 | 21 | 9 | 21 |
| 10 | 0 | 10 | 0 | 10 | 0 | 10 | 0 |
| 11 | 9 | 11 | 9 | 11 | 9 | 11 | 9 |
| 12 | 18 | 12 | 18 | 12 | 18 | 12 | 18 |
| 13 | 27 | 13 | 27 | 13 | 27 | 13 | 27 |
| 14 | 6 | 14 | 6 | 14 | 6 | 14 | 6 |
| 15 | 15 | 15 | 15 | 15 | 15 | 15 | 15 |
| 16 | 24 | 16 | 24 | 16 | 24 | 16 | 24 |
| 17 | 3 | 17 | 3 | 17 | 3 | 17 | 3 |
| 18 | 12 | 18 | 12 | 18 | 12 | 18 | 12 |
| 19 | 21 | 19 | 21 | 19 | 21 | 19 | 21 |
| 20 | 0 | 20 | 0 | 20 | 0 | 20 | 0 |
| 21 | 9 | 21 | 9 | 21 | 9 | 21 | 9 |
| 22 | 18 | 22 | 18 | 22 | 18 | 22 | 18 |
| 23 | 27 | 23 | 27 | 23 | 27 | 23 | 27 |
| 24 | 6 | 24 | 6 | 24 | 6 | 24 | 6 |
| 25 | 15 | 25 | 15 | 25 | 15 | 25 | 15 |
| 26 | 24 | 26 | 24 | 26 | 24 | 26 | 24 |
| 27 | 3 | 27 | 3 | 27 | 3 | 27 | 3 |
| 28 | 12 | 28 | 12 | 28 | 12 | 28 | 12 |
| 29 | 21 | 29 | 21 | 29 | 21 | 29 | 21 |

## The Novienic Table

*Minutes*

| | | | | | | | |
|---|---|---|---|---|---|---|---|
| 00′= | 0°00′ | 15′ = | 2°15′ | 30′ = | 4°30′ | 45′ = | 6°45′ |
| 01 | 0 09 | 16 | 2 24 | 31 | 4 39 | 46 | 6 54 |
| 02 | 0 18 | 17 | 2 33 | 32 | 4 48 | 47 | 7 03 |
| 03 | 0 27 | 18 | 2 42 | 33 | 4 57 | 48 | 7 12 |
| 04 | 0 36 | 19 | 2 51 | 34 | 5 06 | 49 | 7 21 |
| 05 | 0 45 | 20 | 3 00 | 35 | 5 15 | 50 | 7 30 |
| 06 | 0 54 | 21 | 3 09 | 36 | 5 24 | 51 | 7 39 |
| 07 | 1 03 | 22 | 3 18 | 37 | 5 33 | 52 | 7 48 |
| 08 | 1 12 | 23 | 3 27 | 38 | 5 42 | 53 | 7 57 |
| 09 | 1 21 | 24 | 3 36 | 39 | 5 51 | 54 | 8 06 |
| 10 | 1 30 | 25 | 3 45 | 40 | 6 00 | 55 | 8 15 |
| 11 | 1 39 | 26 | 3 54 | 41 | 6 09 | 56 | 8 24 |
| 12 | 1 48 | 27 | 4 03 | 42 | 6 18 | 57 | 8 33 |
| 13 | 1 57 | 28 | 4 12 | 43 | 6 27 | 58 | 8 42 |
| 14 | 2 06 | 29 | 4 21 | 44 | 6 36 | 59 | 8 51 |

## Interpreting the Lunar Return

It was in 1944, to be precise on April 30, that the marked superiority of the sidereal over the tropical version of the solar and lunar revolutions first became manifest. In the years immediately following this revolutionary discovery, under the caption, "The Incidents and Accidents of Astrology," these sidereal versions were first introduced to the astrological public in the pages of the American Federation of Astrologers' *Today's Astrologer,* then edited by Ernest Grant. In 1950, the research director of the Llewellyn Foundation published an excellent brochure on them entitled *Solar and Lunar Returns.* Since July 1953, they have been recently discussed in the Solunars series in *American Astrology*.

When one considers that prior to 1944, solar and lunar returns had all but disappeared from popular astrological literature, it is astonishing how quickly these returns in their new sidereal settings have caught the imagination of many of the leading astrological minds in the world, who find in them the perfect astrological keys to the ensuing future yet devised. The sidereal version of the lunar return has become a firm favourite and constant companion, not only for its consistent reliability, but also because it can be erected in a matter of minutes, especially should a sidereal ephemeris be at hand. It is only necessary to compute the Moon's sidereal longitude to the degree and minute of arc, the longitudes of the Sun and the rest of the planets being required only to the nearest degree.

But for many old-timers in the astrological art, the sidereal version of the lunar return has proven a disappointment. On investigation it has been found these astrologers will persist in trying to interpret the chart according to the rules of horary astrology or according to the system of astrology prevalent in India with its complicated and lengthy list of planetary combinations, known as *yogas*. For their benefit, as for the beginner, the following brief instructions on the successful interpretation of the sidereal lunar return are written.

At the outset, an important word as to the method of computation. Unfortunately some students calculate the tropical lunar return and then reduce it to the sidereal by applying to all the longitudes the vernal point or the *ayanamsa*. This is the wrong procedure, which always gives wrong timing which increases in error according to the age of the native. The correct procedure is outlined in Chapter XIV of this book.

It is most important to realize that the sidereal lunar return (S.L.R.) is a mundane and not a zodiacal chart at all. Except to ascertain the relative strength of the planets in the cosmos (ecliptic), we are not concerned with the zodiac at all! The degrees of the zodiac are inserted on the cusps of the houses for the sake of convenience but have no astrological import. Hence the absurdity of, say, concluding that just because Cancer is rising with its ruler, the Moon, in Sagittarius in the sixth house, that the native will be ill during the ensuing month. This is horary astrology and doesn't apply to lunar returns.

Moreover, the chart being purely mundane in character, zodiacal (ecliptical) aspects do not apply. But as the mundane conjunction and opposition more or less tally with their zodiacal counterparts, these latter may be taken into consideration as well as the zodiacal square when it approximates in value to its mundane equivalent. All other zodiacal aspects such as trines and sextiles should be ignored.

The longer a planet lingers in or near the same zodiacal degree, the more powerful and enduring are its cosmic influences. This is particularly true of the fast-moving bodies, Mercury, Venus and Mars. All of the planets are cosmically puissant when in their first and second stations, particularly the latter, or when they are retrograding in opposition to the Sun or in an inferior conjunction with it. Mercury, Venus and Mars, when rapid in their daily motions, have, cosmically considered, very little influence and their effects are seldom noticed.

Mundanely, the influence of a planet or a luminary is most marked for weal or woe when it is in propinquity to any one of the four angles, and especially the two superior ones, the Ascendant and the cusp of the tenth house. The influence of a planet is enfeebled, almost to the point of extinction, should it be situated midway between adjacent angles, especially those below the horizon. A planet is said to be in propinquity to an angle when it is in mundo within orbs of a pentade (five degrees) on either side of the precise angle. The most acute seats of consciousness are centred at the angles. At these points the native becomes aware of all states of consciousness, including the physical, according to the planet that is on them, if any. For this reason, they alone are the organic nodes of physical pleasure and pain.

For instance, as stated the Moon is the seat of self-consciousness; that is to say it connotes the ego in its negative expression. Should the Sun be configured (orb: a pentade) with the Moon, the native will be highly commended, if not flattered, thereby inflating his ego. Should the Moon also be in propinquity with the angles, he is likely to be personally embraced, decorated or honoured in some way. On the other hand, should the Moon be configured with Mars in the lunar return, he will become the subject of sharp personal criticism, thus puncturing his ego. Should Mars be with Saturn, the attack will be vitriolic. But should the Moon be with Saturn too, or in propinquity to one or other of the four angles, he is liable to be the victim of assault and battery, which could be fatal.

The *ecce homo* (Behold the man!) configuration is, of course, the Moon close to an angle in the lunar return. When this occurs the native becomes the cynosure of all eyes and the chief centre of attraction and interest, as on his wedding day, on the stage, in the ring, in the dock and so forth. On such occasions, knowing all eyes are on him, he is more than usually self-conscious and his person is more exposed and vulnerable. Such a position indicates a personal appearance.

The Sun denotes the positive expression of the ego. It is the significator of fame. Should it be angular and unafflicted in the return, it denotes the native will become famous during the current lunar month in his own circle whether that circle is international or merely parochial. On the other hand, should the Sun be remote from the angles, no distinction will be accorded him during the lunar month.

Wherein his fame will lie depends on the intrinsic nature of the planet in close configuration with the Sun. Should it be the Moon, the native becomes the darling of the crowd, and he waxes in popularity and is liable to be embraced. Should it be configured with Mercury, he will win distinction as a speaker, writer, mathematician or even as a business man. Should it be with Venus, as an Adonis, matinee idol or great lover. Configured with Mars, he wins fame as a conqueror or hero; with Jupiter, as a statesman or judge; with Saturn, as a scientist or natural philosopher; with Uranus, for his unexpected originality; with Neptune, in show-biz or as a clown; with Pluto, as a recluse.

As the Moon is the prime significator in the solar return, so is the Sun the prime significator in the lunar return. Close mundane aspects of transiting planets to the Sun should be considered angular.

It is of the greatest importance to ascertain what natal planet or planets, if any, are transited by the Sun on the date of the lunar return, as such will condition the influence operating that month. Should it closely configure natal Moon on that date, the native will be made much aware of himself as a person, and will be an object of attraction and possibly desire. Liable to be complimented, such a configuration often precipitates the union of the sexes. Should the Sun transit Mercury, the keyword of the month will be work, study, mathematics, mental pursuits, and so forth. Should it transit radical Venus, pleasure will take over the business of the month. Should the Moon be also configured with Venus at birth, then much attention will be lavished on one's wardrobe and toilette, and one may be seen frequenting fashionable salons, the theatre, musical festivals and the like. Should the Sun transit the natal Mars, then the pent-up passions tend to become inflamed and seek an outlet for their release. If frustrated in this endeavour, they may explode in temper and even more violent behaviour should transiting Mars also configure its natal place. Further, should Mars simultaneously configure the Moon, then the native's self-respect is liable to be impugned, thoroughly infuriating him. Such a configuration occurring in the angles may lead to physical violence. Mars is usually represented as the God of War but it is not so well known that in astrology it is also personified by Cupid (Eros) armed with arrow and by Prispus.

The luckiest transit of all is that of the Sun to natal Jupiter. During such a lunar month, the native wins the respect of those who move in the higher cultural levels of society. Should such a transit occur on the Midheaven, the native may receive the accolade. Should natal Moon and Jupiter be mutually configured the native's ego will expand like a balloon. The worst transit to occur is that of the Sun to natal Saturn. Such a configuration spells defeat, rejection, business failure and so forth. And should the Moon and Saturn be natally mutually aspected, the native is liable to sink into the slough of despondency.

The transit of the Sun to Uranus marks an exciting if not thrilling month, replete with every kind of novelty and the society of the young. The solar transit to Neptune inclines the native to commit many follies, leading him into grave trouble. Succumbing to the quest for sensation, and inclined to excess, the onlooker may conclude that he has taken leave of his senses. However, it may be a fruitful time for his musical aspirations, if any. For the transiting of radical Pluto, the native may voluntarily escape from the maddening crowd and seek peace of mind in the privacy of his den or in the country.

The reader should keep in mind that transiting bodies always act centripetally while natal ones always act centrifugally. Thus should Venus when in slow motion transit natal Sun, the native is liable to be shown affection; but should the Sun transit natal Venus, the native tends to be kind and affectionate to others. Again, should transiting Mars, when slow in motion, configure the radical Sun or Moon, the native is liable to be attacked or molested by another, frequently sexually, or else he is attacked by a virus. But on the other hand, should transiting Sun cross natal or progressed Mars the native himself may be tempted to sexually molest an-

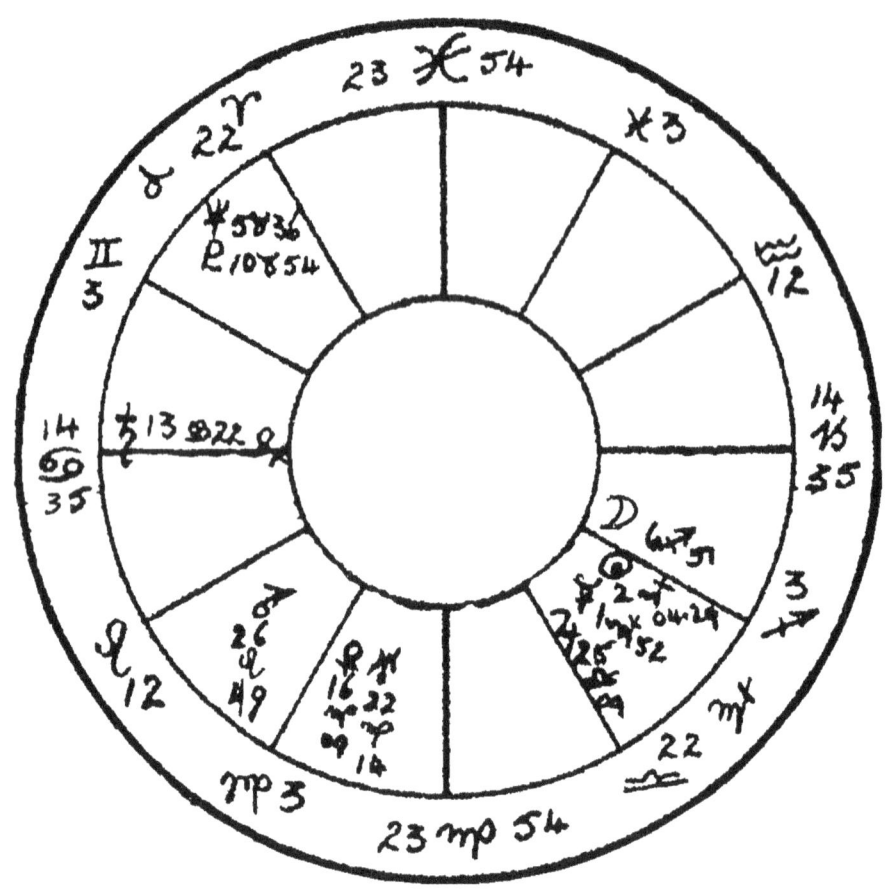

*Chart No. 1, Natal, Field Marshal Lord Montgomery*
*November 17, 1887, 9:17 p.m. GMT, London, Data from Mother*

other. The lunar returns of killers invariably show natal or progressed Mars under the stress of transits at the times of their crimes. Sex crimes have been found to be most prevalent when transiting Venus in one or other of her stations transited the killer's natal Mars!

Perhaps the most famous and convincing of all lunar returns is that of Field Marshal Lord Montgomery for the battle of El Alamein which took place in the Egyptian desert on October 23, 1942. November 4, 1942, found the German army under Rommel in full retreat and General Montgomery a national hero. In a memorable speech Sir Winston Churchill hailed the victory as the turning point of World War II.

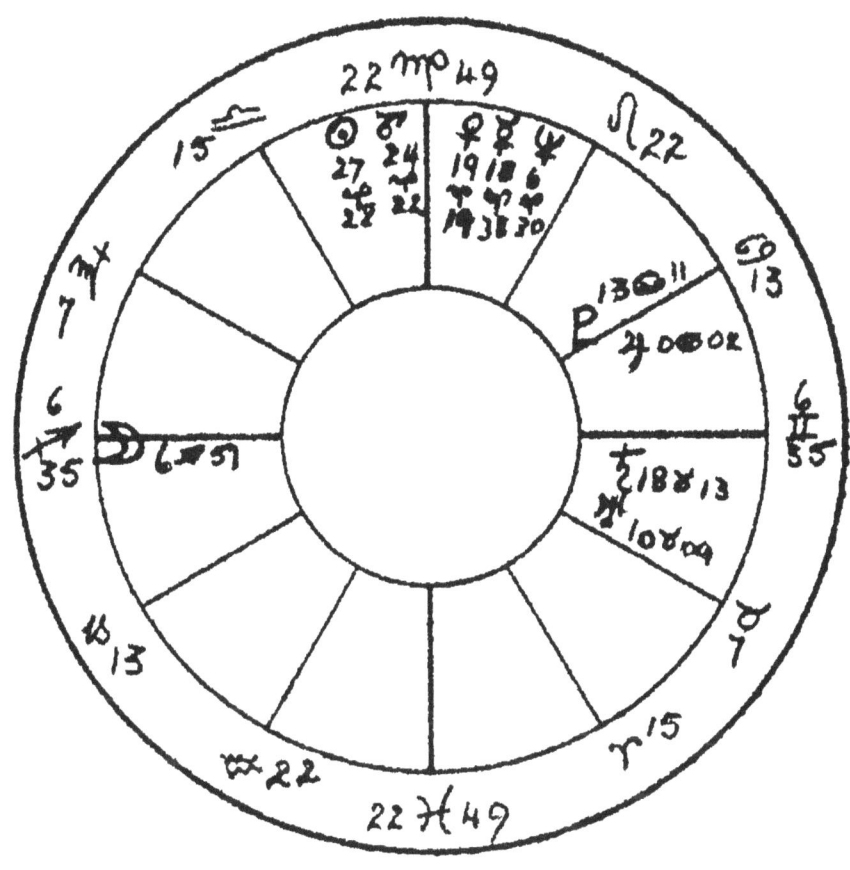

*Chart No. 2, Field Marshall Lord Montgomery*
*Sidereal Lunar Return, El Alamain, October 15, 1942*

There can be no question at all about the authenticity of the General's birth data for his mother gave it as 9:17 p.m. G.M.T., November 17, 1887, at Kennington, London. This is believed to be the time entered in the family bible at the time of his birth. The sidereal version of his geniture is herewith shown in Chart No. 1. Chart No. 2 is the relevant lunar return. It is computed for October 15, 1942, 9:33 a.m. G.M.T. for latitude 30N37 and longitude 28E55. It is an astonishing chart and unquestionably that of a victor. The first thing that strikes the eye is the precise position of natal Uranus on the Midheaven denoting that surprise dispositions and tactics on the part of the general win the day. This is reinforced by the fact that transiting Sun and Mars were close to natal Uranus in this return, to say nothing of transiting Venus. In this battle, Montgomery was actuated by a happy stroke of genius (Uranus). But the Sun and Mars in mutual configurations so close to the M.C. bespeak the conquering hero as well as fame. The precise ecliptical rising of the Moon denoted that the spotlight of the world was focused on his personality and he became hot news. The reader will notice that Neptune was transiting in square to natal Moon, suggesting that the general was more than a little bit excited about his own achievement.

As the seed is to the flower, so is the lunar to the demilunar return. The latter is computed in precisely the same manner as the lunar, save that it is based on the monthly transit of the Moon to that point in the ecliptic diametrically opposite to its natal sidereal longitude.

The demilunar reveals if, and how, the promise of the lunar comes to fruition. Actions undertaken at the inception of the latter will render the native famous within his sphere, should the Sun be angular in the demilunar. Should the Moon be angular in this chart, and not under the check of the malefics, then like the incoming tide, the native's chest will swell with bashful pride as he is applauded by the public. But should an afflicted Moon hold the angles, the native thus exposed to unsympathetic eyes will feel highly self-conscious, embarrassed, and perhaps humiliated, wishing the earth would open and engulf him in the void.

Should Saturn be angular in the demilunar, and Jupiter cadent, then the fair hopes and promise of the lunar will be blighted. Or should Pluto be there, such promises may go contrariwise, much to the native's shock and dismay.

On the other hand, should the month open with an evil lunar, but a good demilunar, then out of evil will emerge good and the native will live happily for the rest of the month.

# Appenix

## Calculation of Planets In Mundo

By calculating in mundo we obtain the culmination, rising or setting of the body of the planet and not its longitudinal position. With planets which have considerable latitude, such as Pluto, Moon and Venus, this position can differ considerably from the mundane position. The Sun has no latitude.

The calculation is not difficult but does necessitate the use of logarithms. It is fortunately not necessary to understand logarithms in order to use them. If you have never used logarithms, get a friend to show you how it is done.

As an example, we shall use Pluto, which has the greatest potential difference between the two positions. We shall calculate the times of culminating, rising and setting of Pluto on July 1, 1962.

We have first to find the right ascension, or R.A., of the planet.

As sidereal time can also be called R.A.M.C., it is apparent that a planet culminates when its R.A. is the same as the sidereal time of the map. R.A. can be expressed in hours and minutes or in degrees and minutes, the first figure being obtainable from the second by dividing by 15 since 15 degrees equals one hour. Unfortunately, few ephemerides give the R.A. It is given in the *Nautical Almanac* and in Stahl's sidereal ephemerides, where it is given in degrees. When your ephemeris does not give it, our first task is to calculate it.

For planets which have latitude, the formula reads:

$$\cos A = \frac{\cos b \cos l}{\cos d}$$

where "A" is the required R.A., "b" the latitude of the planet, "d" the declination, and "l" the tropical longitude.

There is one complication. If the tropical longitude falls between 0 Cancer and 0 Libra or between 0 Capricorn and 0 Aries, 90-180 or 270-360 degrees, the log sin of "l" must be substituted for the log cos and the sum of the logarithms will be the log sin of the R.A.

We will use Raphael's tropical ephemeris for 1962. On July 1, Pluto's tropical longitude will be 7 Virgo 58, latitude 13N03 and declination 20N38. We require a four-figure logarithmic table giving log sines, cosines and tangents. We note that the longitude of Pluto falls between 90 and 180 degrees; therefore, the log sin must be used instead of the log cos for its longitude and the sum.

Our calculations therefore read:

Log cos 13° 03'      9.9888
Log sin 67° 58'      9.9671  (67° 58' is the distance from 0° Cancer)

Add                  9.9559
Log cos 20° 38'      9.9714
Log sin 74° 48'      9.9845

We have obtained the figure of 74° 48' by looking up our result 9.9845 in the log sin tables. This is therefore the R.A. of the planet measured from 0 Cancer or 90 degrees R.A. To it we must add this 90 degrees, obtaining 164° 48' as the R.A. of the planet in degrees. Stahl gives the same figure.

If it is wished to turn this figure into hours, minutes and seconds, divide by 15, obtaining 10h 59m 12s. If we look up this sidereal time in any tropical ephemeris, we shall see that the M.C. is approximately 13 Virgo 30 so that Pluto culminates when this longitude is on the M.C. As the tropical longitude of Pluto is 7 Virgo 58, there is a difference of about five and a half degrees between the two positions. Pluto, therefore, with its north latitude, culminates later than its longitudinal degree. The point of lower culmination (I.C.) will be 13 Pisces 30. The corresponding sidereal degree will be about 19 Aquarius. If you wish, you can get these figures closer by interpolation.

We now have to find the times of rising and setting, using the R.A. which we have calculated or taken from tables.

The formula for the rising and setting is:

$$\sin a/d = \tan g \tan d$$

where "a/d" is the ascensional difference, "g" the geocentric latitude of the place, and "d" the declination.

If the native resides north of the equator and the declination is north, the a/d will be positive. But if the declination is south or negative, the a/d will be negative. If the native resides in the southern hemisphere, these signs will be reversed.

This is the first part of the calculation with which we shall now deal. The geocentric latitude of London is 51N21.

tan 51° 21'   0.0971
tan 20° 38'   0.5758
sin 28° 06'   9.6729

We obtain this figure, 28° 06', by looking up 9.6729 in the log sin table.

There is a second part to this calculation. To find the planet's semiarc, (s/a), add the a/d to 90 if it is positive, and subtract it if it is negative. London is north of the equator and the declination being north the a/d is positive. We therefore add the a/d to 90.

```
         90
plus   28 06
       118 06  which is the planet's semiarc (s/a)
```

The R.A.M.C. of a planet rising is the R.A. minus the semiarc.

```
Pluto's R.A.   164° 48'
Semiarc       -118 06
                46 42
```

Divided by 15, we have 3h 06m 48s as the sidereal time of rising.

At this time, sidereal 5 Leo 30 rises at London and Pluto with it. At this time, the longitude of Pluto is 13° Leo 45', a difference of more than eight degrees. Pluto rises in mundo 48 minutes earlier than it appears to do from its ephemeris degree.

At the present time, when Pluto has north latitude and we are considering the northern hemisphere, the difference when setting will be much greater. Calculate the July 1, 1962 position:

The R.A.M.C. of a planet setting is R.A. plus semiarc.

```
Pluto R.A.     164° 48'
Plus semiarc   118 06
               282 54
```

Divided by 15, this gives 18h 51m 36s at which time the sidereal degree 5 Libra 45 sets in London. As at this time the longitude of Pluto is 13 Leo 45, it will be seen that there is a difference of no less than 51 degrees. With its north latitude, Pluto will therefore set at London with a longitudinal degree of 5 Libra 45 or 1h 30m later than its ephemeris degree. This large difference is due to the fact that with the present position of Pluto we have a constellation of short ascension rising. For less extreme latitudes the difference will not be so great. At the equator there will be no difference. When we are dealing with places south of the equator these differences will be reversed, the greatest difference being when Pluto is rising.

To show how easy and quick it is once you have mastered the technique, your work sheet for the same calculation for New York can look like this.

| New York geoc. | Lat. 40N34 | 9.9325 | | |
|---|---|---|---|---|
| | Decl. 20N38 | 9.5758 | | |
| | | 9.5083 | 18 48 | |
| | | | 90 | |
| | | | 108 48 | |

| Rise | 164 48 | Set | 164 48 |
|---|---|---|---|
| Minus | 108 48 | Plus | 108 48 |
| | 56 00 = Leo 9 | | 273 36 = Virgo 12 |

If you are using Stahl's ephemerides, it is unnecessary to divide by 15 to get hours as these ephemerides show the R.A.

## Calculating Lunar Configurations

In early editions of Raphael's ephemerides there are no aspectarians, and many ephemerides of today do not include the times of lunar configurations. The following example will show how they can easily be calculated.

Example: In the Capsolar of 1918, the Moon by progression was applying to the conjunction of progressed Venus. At what time did this occur. The ephemeris used is a Greenwich mean noon ephemeris. D.M. is the abbreviation for diurnal motion.

| Jan. 14 Moon Aq. | 14° 42' | Jan. 14 Venus Aq. | 27° 50' |
|---|---|---|---|
| Jan. 15 Moon Aq. | 29   27 | Jan. 15 Venus Aq. | 28   03 |
| | | | |
| Moon's D.M. | 14   45 | Venus D.M. | 0   13 |
| Subtract Venus D.M. | 00   13 | | |
| | | | |
| M | 14   02 | | |
| Jan. 14 Moon Aq. | 14° 42' | | |
| Jan. 14 Venus Aq. | 27   50 | | |
| Difference | 13   08 | | |
| | | | |
| Difference | 13° 08' | Diurnal log | 0.26184 |
| M | 14   32 | | 0.21785 |
| G.M.T. 21h 41m | | | 9.04399 |

N.B. If the planet is retrograding, it must be added to the D.M. of the Moon.

If the Moon's motion were regular during 24 hours, the time obtained by this formula would be exact. The Moon's motion is, however, never regular during the course of the day. The error will rarely exceed two and a half days in the date of maturation.

## Paranatellonta

Reference has been made in this book to the formation known as *paranatellonta,* a word meaning planets being simultaneously on two succeeding angles. As these are not apparent at a glance, we shall show how they are calculated. They are of great importance both in birth maps and in solar and lunar returns. We shall take as our example the solar return of President Kennedy for 1962.

Place each planet in turn on the four angles and note for each position the corresponding M.C. or Ascendant. Thus:

Saturn Capricorn 17
  on
| M.C. | Asc. | 9 Taurus | |
| I.C. | Asc. | 11 Libra | Just out of orb for paran |
| Asc. | M.C. | 6 Scorpio | |
| Desc. | M.C. | 7 Aries conj. Mars | Saturn paran Mars |

Mars 7 Aries
  on
| M.C. | Asc. | 17 Cancer opp. Saturn | Mars paran Saturn |
| I.C. | Asc. | 13 Sag. opp. Venus | Mars paran Venus |
| Asc. | M.C. | 23 Sagittarius | |
| Desc. | M.C. | 12 Cancer | Just out of orb for paran |

Is Jupiter in paran with any other planet in this solar return?

Jupiter 17 Aquarius
  on
| M.C. | Asc. | 9 Gemini | |
| I.C. | Asc. | 4 Scorpio | |
| Asc. | M.C. | 26 Scorpio | |
| Desc. | M.C. | 14 Taurus 30 conj. Sun | Jupiter is paran Sun |

In his solar return for 1962, Mars is therefore in a paran with Saturn and Venus, a paran which seems to fit the facts. But fortunately, during the same year the Sun is in a paran to Jupiter, a paran which preserves one in trouble to say the least.

Although it is outside the scope of this chapter, nevertheless it is interesting to note that the *navamsa* map for this solar return, which would not be neglected by any self-respecting Indian astrologer, has Mars conjunct Saturn.

## Precessing

If a planet has a certain right ascension and declination at birth, its birth position will not have the same R.A. and declination for any subsequent year because of precession. So the processes of determining the true R.A. and declination of a natal or progressed planet for any date after birth is called "precessing." Precessing really means expunging the precession that has accumulated from the date of the radix to the required date. Because precession is always negative, the expunging process is always additive to cancel out the accumulated precession.

With regard to the Sidereal Natal Quotidian (S.N.Q.), the M.S. at birth must be precessed before the S.N.Q. can be correctly computed. Fortunately, this involves no computation, as the M.S. of the current S.S.R. is the precessed M.S. of the S.N.Q. Thus, in the nativity of John Kennedy the natal M.S. is 4h 27m 04s. But for the date of his election to the presidency, it will have to be precessed, which gives its value for 1960 as 4h 29m 26s, which is the M.S. of the S.S.R. for 1960. The M.S. progresses at the mean rate of 3.3 seconds per annum. Of course, in calculating the Tropical Natal Quotidian, or T.N.Q., the natal M.S. is used.

In connection with the planets, the following formulae are recommended by James Hynes:

$$\cos T = \sin e \cos L'$$
$$\tan (x - b) = \tan e \sin L'$$
$$x = (x - b) + b$$
$$\cot (A + y) = \cos e \cot L'$$
$$\tan y = \cos T \tan x$$
$$A = (A+y) - y$$
$$\cos d = \cos x / \cos y$$

These formulae look complicated, but they are in fact quite simple and straightforward, giving accurate results, even when the latitude is quite small. Before exemplifying them, however, it should be mentioned that whereas the R.A. and declination are tropical coordinates, i.e., they are affected by precession, celestial latitude is a sidereal coordinate, and is thus not so affected. In the course of time, latitude is affected by the Sun's proper motion in space, which alters the position of the ecliptic which, in its turn, alters the latitude. But, in a period of 1,000 years the movement is so minute as to be negligible, and so, to all intents and purposes, the celestial latitude can be taken, for a given epoch, as being fixed. In the foregoing formulae, "e" is the obliquity of the ecliptic (for 1961 23° 27'), "L'" the precessed tropical longitude of the planet, "b" its latitude, "A" its new R.A. and "d" its new declination.

At the time of President Kennedy's birth, the tropical longitude of Jupiter was 23 Taurus 04 (53° 04'); its declination was + 17° 44', its latitude was 0° 50', and its radical R.A. 50° 54'. Let us now find its R.A. and declination for January 1, 1961.

| | | |
|---|---|---|
| Date of birth, 1917, May 29 | S.V.P. Pisces | 6° 24' 30.8" |
| Date of birth, 1961, January 1 | S.V.P. Pisces | 5 48 21.4 |
| Accrued Precession | | 0 36 09.4 |
| Jupiter's Tropical Long. at Date of Birth | | 53 04 |
| L' = Jupiter's Precessed Long | | 53 40 |

```
e  23°7.5 sin 9.59969    e   23 27.5 tan 9.63710    e   2327.5 cos 9.96259
L' 53 40  cos 9.77268    L'  53 40   sin 9.90611    L'  53 40   cot 9.86656

   T  cos 9.37237 (x-b) 19 15  tan 9.54321  (A+y)   55 59  cot 9.82915
   x  tan 9.51819    b       0 50

y + 4°36'  tan 8.89056   x   18 25  cos 9.9775860  (A+y) 55°59'
                         y    4 36  cos 9.9985988    y    4 35
                         d+  17 41  cos 9.9789874    A   51 23
```

The above are the logarithms for the trigonometric functions. Hence, for January 1, 1961, the R.A. was 51°30', or 3h 26m 00s in sidereal time, and the declination north 17°53'.

As can be seen, the above computation is not at all difficult but the following points should be remembered: "b" must always be added algebraically to (x-b) while "y" must always be subtracted algebraically from (A+y), as in the manner for obtaining the Equation of Time when finding the increment for the P.S.S.R. Note too, the log cos y subtracted from the log cos x, and the remainder will be the log cos of the declination, which will take the same sign as "x". If "x" is plus, "d" will be plus, but if negative, "d" will be negative.

## Notes on Tables

### Table 1

This table gives for the beginning of every Julian century from B.C. 4001 (-4000) to A.D. 2100, the mean sidereal longitude of the vernal point, i.e., the "0 Aries" of the modern tropical zodiac, reckoned from the beginning of the sidereal zodiac and expressed in decimals of a degree.

All dates B.C. must be converted to their astronomical equivalents by subtracting 1 from the year number and then prefixing a minus sign to the remainder, thus:

> B.C. 2767 becomes - 2766 (astronomical)
> B.C.  786 becomes -  785
> B.C.    1 becomes -    0

Rule 1: To fmd the mean S.V.P. for the beginning of any intermediate year, multiply the intermediate years (treated as a decimal of a century) by "d" and deduct from the mean S.V.P. for the century.

Example 1: Find the mean S.V.P. for A.D. 1776.

$1776 = 1700 + 76$

|  |  | S.V.P. |
|---|---|---|
| A.D. 1700 |  | 339.447 |
| 76 | 0.76 x d = 0.76 x (-1.395) | 1.060 |
| A.D. 1776 |  | 338.387 |

Rule 2: In the case of years B.C. which are always negative, subtract the intermediate years from 100, multiply by "d" and deduct from the S.V.P. for the previous century.

Example 2: Find the mean S.V.P. for the year beginning -2766, i.e., B.C. 2767. Intermediate years 66 deducted from 100 = 34. Therefore, -2800 + 34 = -2766.

|  |  | S.V.P. |
|---|---|---|
| - 2800 |  | 41.591 |
| 34 | 0.34 x (- 1.368) | -0.465 |
| - 2766 |  | 41.126 |

Example 3: In what year did the Piscean Age commence? Theoretically, the Piscean Age commenced when the S.V.P. (the movement of which is always retrograde) leaves 0 Aries or enters 30 Pisces, which is the same thing.

A.D. 200     d = -1.386     S.V.P. 0.300

Then 100 x 0.300 / 1.386 = 21.6 years + 200 = A.D. 221.6

Known as the Zero Year, the sidereal and modern tropical zodiacs therefore coincided in the middle of 221 A.D. This was less than a century later than the time when the *Almagest* and *Tetrabiblos* attributed to Claudius Ptolemy, and the *Apotelesmatica* attributed to the Pseudo-Manetho were written. Hence to all intents and purposes the zodiac of Claudius Ptolemy and the Pseudo-Manetho was sidereal with *ayanamsa* or difference in longitude between the two zodiacs being only about one degree. Some 200 years earlier than this Zero

Year, the Roman astrologer, Manilius, penned his immortal *Astronomicon.* Using the same simple method of linear proportion, the date when the Arian Age commenced can also be computed from Table I.

**Table II**

In the compilation of astronomical tables, it has been found in many cases to be more convenient to express minutes and seconds of a degree, or an hour as a decimal of a degree or hour, as the case may be. Table II will facilitate the reader in making the necessary reduction, and vice versa.

Example 5: Reduce the mean S.V.P. 338.387° for A.D. 1776 into minutes and seconds of a degree.

```
A.D. 1776 Mean S.V:P.          338.387
(Example 1)
                        23' -  .3833
                        C/F    .0037

                        B/f    .0037
                        13"    .6666
                               .0001
```

Hence, the mean S.V.P. for the beginning of A.D. 1776 was 338° 23'13".

**Table III**

This gives for the beginning of every tropical year, actually the Besselian year, which begins when the right ascension of the Mean Sun (M.S.) is precisely 18h 40m, or 280°, usually about January 1, from A.D. 1800 to A.D. 2000, inclusive, the mean longitude of the synetic vernal point (S.V.P.), i.e., the "0 Aries" of the tropical zodiac, in terms of the sidereal zodiac. While most astrologers are aware that this point retrogrades along the path of the ecliptic at the rate of one degree in about 71.5 years, it is not so well known that this same point, from which the modern tropical zodiac takes its origin, is not a clearly defined point in space, albeit mathematical, but a fuzzy, indistinct position that sways in irregular fashion, backwards and forwards, reckoned from it. It follows that these longitudes are also blurred and irregular in motion, which will be observed when they are computed to fractions of a second of an arc. This oscillating fuzziness is caused by the long-time and short-time periods of nutation (nodding), both solar and lunar, and before the true sidereal longitude of the S.V.P. can be found from its mean position, the latter has to be corrected for such fuzziness. For the purpose of this exposition, the short terms in nutation can be disregarded, as they make only a fractional difference of a second of an arc. But the long terms in nutation do make a substantial difference, sufficient to cause appreciable errors in the calculation of solar returns, where a deviation of only 10" of an arc in Sun's longitude is equivalent to a corresponding error of over four minutes in time.

To ascertain the true sidereal longitude of the S.V.P. three corrections have to be applied to its mean position, namely annual precession, and solar and lunar nutation.

**Tables IV and V**

Given the mean sidereal longitude of the S.V.P. at the beginning of the year, the M.S. and the mean node (M.N.) it is quite a simple matter to obtain the true S.V.P.

Example: To calculate for the birth of Sir Winston Churchill who was born on November 30, 1874, at the speculative time of 5:30 p.m.

```
From ephemeris S.T. noon      16h 36m 45s
Correction for 5h 30m                  55
Mean Sun (M.S.)               16   37   40
```

Table III 1874, Jan. 1. Mean S.V.P.    Pisces 7° 01' 08.3"
Table IV 1st Correction
   Argument M.S. 16h 37m 40s
     M.S. 16h 30m    - 44.72
     M.S. 16h 40m    - 45.15
Then by simple proportion the correction for 16h 37m 40s is    45.05
                                                             7 00 23.25

**Table V 2nd Correction**

Argument: Mean Node 24 Aries 21 = Long. 24° 21'

        M.N. 24° + 6.85"
        M.N. 25° + 7.12"

        Correction for 24° 21'        +9.45
        Synetic Vernal Point   Pisces 7 00 32.7

It should be noted that in Table IV the first correction is always negative or subtractive, whereas in Table V it will be positive or additive when the mean node is between 0° and 180° but negative or subtractive when it is between 180° and 360°. In this table the argument is the zodiacal longitude of the mean node.

## Table I
*Mean Sidereal Longitude of the Synetic Vernal Point for the Beginning of Each Century (Julian)*

| G | Century | S.V.P. | d | G | Century | S.V.P. | d |
|---|---------|--------|---|---|---------|--------|---|
| 32 | -4000 | 57.9S3° |  | 20 | -2400 | 36.117° |  |
|  |  |  | -1.360 |  |  |  | -1.370 |
| 31 | -3900 | 56.S93 |  | 19 | -2300 | 34.747 |  |
|  |  |  | -1.361 |  |  |  | -1.371 |
| 30 | -3800 | S5.232 |  | 18 | -2200 | 33.376 |  |
|  |  |  | -1.362 |  |  |  | -1.371 |
| 29 | -3700 | S3.870 |  | 17 | -2100 | 32.005 |  |
|  |  |  | -1.362 |  |  |  | -1.372 |
| 29 | -3600 | 52.S08 |  | 17 | -2000 | 30.633 |  |
|  |  |  | -1.362 |  |  |  | -1.372 |
| 28 | -3500 | 51.146 |  | 16 | -1900 | 39.261 |  |
|  |  |  | -1.363 |  |  |  | -1.373 |
| 27 | -3400 | 49.783 |  | 15 | -1800 | 27.888 |  |
|  |  |  | -1.364 |  |  |  | -1.373 |
| 26 | -3300 | 48.419 |  | 14 | -1700 | 26.515 |  |
|  |  |  | -1.365 |  |  |  | -1.375 |
| 26 | -3200 | 47.0S4 |  | 14 | -1600 | 2S.140 |  |
|  |  |  | -1.365 |  |  |  | -1.375 |
| 25 | -3100 | 45.689 |  | 13 | -1500 | 23.765 |  |
|  |  |  | -1.365 |  |  |  | -1.375 |
| 24 | -3000 | 44.324 |  | 12 | -1400 | 22.390 |  |
|  |  |  | -1.366 |  |  |  | -1.376 |
| 23 | -2900 | 42.9S8 |  | 11 | -1300 | 21.014 |  |
|  |  |  | -1.367 |  |  |  | -1.377 |
| 23 | -2800 | 41.591 |  | 11 | -1200 | 19.637 |  |
|  |  |  | -1.368 |  |  |  | -1.377 |
| 22 | -2700 | 40.223 |  | 10 | -1100 | 18.260 |  |
|  |  |  | -1.368 |  |  |  | -1.378 |
| 21 | -2600 | 38.8S5 |  | 9 | -1000 | 16.882 |  |
|  |  |  | -1.369 |  |  |  | -1.378 |
| 20 | -2500 | 37.486 |  | 8 | - 900 | 15504 |  |
|  |  |  | -1.369 |  |  |  |  |
| 8 | - 900 | 15.504 |  | -4 | + 700 | 353.364 |  |
|  |  |  | -1.380 |  |  |  | -1.389 |

| G | Century | S.V.P. | d | G | Century | S.V.P. | d |
|---|---|---|---|---|---|---|---|
| 8 | -800 | 14.124 | | -4 | +800 | 351.975 | |
| | | | -1.379 | | | | -1.390 |
| 7 | -700 | 12.745 | | -5 | +900 | 350.585 | |
| | | | -1.381 | | | | -1.390 |
| 6 | -600 | 11.364 | | -6 | +1000 | 349.195 | |
| | | | -1.381 | | | | -1.391 |
| 5 | -500 | 9.983 | | -7 | +1100 | 347.804 | |
| | | | -1.381 | | | | -1.391 |
| 5 | -400 | 8.602 | | -7 | +1200 | 346.413 | |
| | | | -1.382 | | | | -1.392 |
| 4 | -300 | 7.220 | | -8 | +1300 | 345.021 | |
| | | | -1.383 | | | | -1.393 |
| 3 | -200 | 5.837 | | -9 | +1400 | 343.628 | |
| | | | -1.384 | | | | -1.393 |
| 2 | -100 | 4.453 | | -10 | +1500 | 342.235 | |
| | | | -1.384 | | | | -1,394 |
| 2 | A.D. 0 | 3.069 | | -10 | +1600 | 340.841 | |
| | | | -1.384 | | | | -1.394 |
| 1 | +100 | 1.685 | | -11 | +1700 | 339,447 | |
| | | | -1.385 | | | | -1.395 |
| 0 | +200 | 0.300 | | -12 | +1800 | 338,052 | |
| | | | -1.386 | | | | -1.396 |
| -1 | +300 | 358.914 | | -13 | +1900 | 336,656 | |
| | | | -1.387 | | | | -1,396 |
| -1 | +400 | 357.527 | | -13 | +2000 | 335.260 | |
| | | | -1.387 | | | | -1.397 |
| -2 | +500 | 356.140 | | -14 | +2100 | 333.863 | |
| | | | -1.388 | | | | |
| -3 | +600 | 354.752 | | | 1950 | 335.958 | |
| | | | -1.388 | | | | |

## Table II
*Reduction of Minutes and Seconds of Arc to Decimals of a Degree and Vice Versa*

|    | Minutes | Seconds |    | Minutes | Seconds |
|----|---------|---------|----|---------|---------|
| 1  | .0167°  | .0003°  | 31 | .5167°  | .0086°  |
| 2  | .0333   | .0006   | 32 | .5333   | .0089   |
| 3  | .0500   | .0008   | 33 | .5500   | .0092   |
| 4  | .0667   | .0011   | 34 | .5667   | .0095   |
| 5  | .0833   | .0014   | 35 | .5833   | .0097   |
| 6  | .1000   | .0017   | 36 | .6000   | .0100   |
| 7  | .1167   | .0019   | 37 | .6167   | .0103   |
| 8  | .1333   | .0022   | 38 | .6333   | .0106   |
| 9  | .1500   | .0025   | 39 | .6500   | .0108   |
| 10 | .1667   | .0028   | 40 | .6667   | .0111   |
| 11 | .1833   | .0031   | 41 | .6833   | .0114   |
| 12 | .2000   | .0033   | 42 | .7000   | .0117   |
| 13 | .2167   | .0036   | 43 | .7167   | .0120   |
| 14 | .2333   | .0039   | 44 | .7233   | .0122   |
| 15 | .2500   | .0042   | 45 | .7500   | .0125   |
| 16 | .2667   | .0044   | 46 | .7667   | .0128   |
| 17 | .2833   | .0047   | 47 | .7833   | .0131   |
| 18 | .3000   | .0050   | 48 | .8000   | .0133   |
| 19 | .3167   | .0053   | 49 | .8167   | .0136   |
| 20 | .3333   | .0055   | 50 | .8333   | .0139   |
| 21 | .3500   | .0058   | 51 | .8500   | .0142   |
| 22 | .3667   | .0061   | 52 | .8667   | .0145   |
| 23 | .3833   | .0064   | 53 | .8833   | .0147   |
| 24 | .4000   | .0067   | 54 | .9000   | .0150   |
| 25 | .4167   | .0070   | 55 | .9167   | .0153   |
| 26 | .4333   | .0072   | 56 | .9333   | .0156   |
| 27 | .4500   | .0075   | 57 | .9500   | .0158   |
| 28 | .4667   | .0078   | 58 | .9667   | .0161   |
| 29 | .4833   | .0081   | 59 | .9833   | .0164   |
| 30 | .5000   | .0083   | 60 | 1.0000  | .0167   |

## Table III

*The mean sidereal longitude in Pisces of the S.V.P. for January 1 (actually for the beginning of the Besselian Year), for each year from 1800 to 2000 A.D., inclusive.*

| Year | Longitude | Year | Longitude | Year | Longitude |
|---|---|---|---|---|---|
| 1800 | 8° 03′06.3″ | 1834 | 7° 34′38.2″ | 1868 | 7° 06′10.8″ |
| 1801 | 8  02 16.0 | 1835 | 7  33 47.9 | 1869 | 7  05 20.6 |
| 1802 | 8  01 25.8 | 1836 | 7  32 57.7 | 1870 | 7  04 29.3 |
| 1803 | 8  00 35.6 | 1837 | 7  32 07.5 | 1871 | 7   03 39.1 |
| 1804 | 7  59 45.3 | 1838 | 7  31 17.2 | 1872 | 7  02 48.8 |
| 1805 | 7  58 55.1 | 1839 | 7  30 27.0 | 1873 | 7  01 58.6 |
| 1806 | 7  58 04.9 | 1840 | 7  29 36.7 | 1874 | 7  01 08.3 |
| 1807 | 7  57 14.6 | 1841 | 7  28 46.5 | 1875 | 7  00 18.1 |
| 1808 | 7  56 24.4 | 1842 | 7  27 56.2 | 1876 | 6  59 27.8 |
| 1809 | 7  55 34.2 | 1843 | 7  27 06.0 | 1877 | 6  58 37.6 |
| 1810 | 7  54 43.9 | 1844 | 7  26 15.7 | 1878 | 6  57 47.3 |
| 1811 | 7  53 53.7 | 1845 | 7  25 25.5 | 1879 | 6  56 57.1 |
| 1812 | 7  53 03.4 | 1846 | 7  24 35.3 | 1880 | 6  56 06.8 |
| 1813 | 7  52 13.2 | 1847 | 7  23 45.0 | 1881 | 6  55 16.6 |
| 1814 | 7  51 23.0 | 1848 | 7  22 54.8 | 1882 | 6  54 26.3 |
| 1815 | 7  50 32.7 | 1849 | 7  22  04.5 | 1883 | 6  53 36.1 |
| 1816 | 7  49 42.5 | 1850 | 7  21 14.3 | 1884 | 6  52 45.8 |
| 1817 | 7  48 52.3 | 1851 | 7  20 24.0 | 1885 | 6  51 55.6 |
| 1818 | 7  48 02.0 | 1852 | 7  19 33.8 | 1886 | 6  51 05.3 |
| 1819 | 7  47 11.8 | 1853 | 7  18 43.5 | 1887 | 6  50 15.0 |
| 1820 | 7  46 21.5 | 1854 | 7  17 53.3 | 1888 | 6  49 24.8 |
| 1821 | 7  45 31.3 | 1855 | 7  17 03.1 | 1889 | 6  48 34.5 |
| 1822 | 7  44 41.1 | 1856 | 7  16 12.8 | 1890 | 6  47 44.3 |
| 1823 | 7  43 50.8 | 1857 | 7  15 22.6 | 1891 | 6  46 54.0 |
| 1824 | 7  43 00.6 | 1858 | 7  14 32.3 | 1892 | 6  46 03.8 |
| 1825 | 7  42 10.3 | 1859 | 7  13 43.1 | 1893 | 6  45 13.5 |
| 1826 | 7  41 20.1 | 1860 | 7  12 51.8 | 1894 | 6  44 23.3 |
| 1827 | 7  40 29.9 | 1861 | 7  12 01.6 | 1895 | 6  43 33.0 |
| 1828 | 7  39 39.6 | 1862 | 7  11 11.3 | 1896 | 6  42 42.8 |
| 1829 | 7  38 49.3 | 1863 | 7  10 21.1 | 1897 | 6  41 52.5 |
| 1830 | 7  37 59.1 | 1864 | 7  09 30.8 | 1898 | 6  41 02.3 |
| 1831 | 7  37 08.9 | 1865 | 7  08 40.6 | 1899 | 6  40 12.0 |
| 1832 | 7  36 18.7 | 1866 | 7  07 50.3 | 1900 | 6  39 21.7 |
| 1833 | 7  35 28.4 | 1867 | 7  07 00.1 | 1901 | 6  38 31.5 |
| 1902 | 6  37 41.2 | 1940 | 6  05 51.3 | 1978 | 5  34 01.1 |

| | | | | | | | | | |
|---|---|---|---|---|---|---|---|---|---|
| 1903 | 6 | 36 51.0 | | 1941 | 6 | 05 01.0 | | 1979 | 5 | 33 10.8 |
| 1904 | 6 | 36 00.7 | | 1942 | 6 | 04 10.8 | | 1980 | 5 | 32 20.5 |
| 1905 | 6 | 35 10.5 | | 1943 | 6 | 03 20.5 | | 1981 | 5 | 31 30.2 |
| 1906 | 6 | 34 20.2 | | 1944 | 6 | 02 30.2 | | 1982 | 5 | 30 40.0 |
| 1907 | 6 | 33 29.9 | | 1945 | 6 | 01 40.0 | | 1983 | 5 | 29 49.7 |
| 1908 | 6 | 32 39.7 | | 1946 | 6 | 00 49.7 | | 1984 | 5 | 28 59.4 |
| 1909 | 6 | 31 49.4 | | 1947 | 5 | 59 59.4 | | 1985 | 5 | 28 09.1 |
| 1910 | 6 | 30 59.2 | | 1948 | 5 | 59 09.2 | | 1986 | 5 | 27 18.9 |
| 1911 | 6 | 30 08.9 | | 1949 | 5 | 58 18.9 | | 1987 | 5 | 26 28.6 |
| 1912 | 6 | 29 18.6 | | 1950 | 5 | 57 28.6 | | 1988 | 5 | 25 38.3 |
| 1913 | 6 | 28 28.4 | | 1951 | 5 | 56 38.4 | | 1989 | 5 | 24 48.0 |
| 1914 | 6 | 27 38.1 | | 1952 | 5 | 55 48.1 | | 1990 | 5 | 23 57.8 |
| 1915 | 6 | 26 47.9 | | 1953 | 5 | 54 57.8 | | 1991 | 5 | 23 07.5 |
| 1916 | 6 | 25 57.6 | | 1954 | 5 | 54 07.6 | | 1992 | 5 | 22 17.2 |
| 1917 | 6 | 25 07.3 | | 1955 | 5 | 53 17.3 | | 1993 | 5 | 21 26.9 |
| 1918 | 6 | 24 17.1 | | 1956 | 5 | 52 27.0 | | 1994 | 5 | 20 36.6 |
| 1919 | 6 | 23 26.8 | | 1957 | 5 | 51 36.8 | | 1995 | 5 | 19 46.4 |
| 1920 | 6 | 22 36.6 | | 1958 | 5 | 50 46.5 | | 1996 | 5 | 18 56.1 |
| 1921 | 6 | 21 46.3 | | 1959 | 5 | 49 56.2 | | 1997 | 5 | 18 05.8 |
| 1922 | 6 | 20 56.0 | | 1960 | 5 | 49 06.0 | | 1998 | 5 | 17 15.5 |
| 1923 | 6 | 20 05.8 | | 1961 | 5 | 48 15.7 | | 1999 | 5 | 16 25.3 |
| 1924 | 6 | 19 15.5 | | 1962 | 5 | 47 25.4 | | 2000 | 5 | 15 35.9 |
| 1925 | 6 | 18 25.3 | | 1963 | 5 | 46 35.1 | | 2001 | 5 | 15.01.0 |
| 1926 | 6 | 17 35.0 | | 1964 | 5 | 45 44.9 | | 2002 | 5 | 14 11.0 |
| 1927 | 6 | 16 44.7 | | 1965 | 5 | 44 54.6 | | 2003 | 5 | 13 20.0 |
| 1928 | 6 | 15 54.5 | | 1966 | 5 | 44 04.3 | | 2004 | 5 | 12 26.0 |
| 1929 | 6 | 15 04.2 | | 1967 | 5 | 43 14.1 | | 2005 | 5 | 11 31.0 |
| 1930 | 6 | 14 13.9 | | 1968 | 5 | 42 23.8 | | 2006 | 5 | 10 35.0 |
| 1931 | 6 | 13 23.7 | | 1969 | 5 | 41 33.5 | | 2007 | 5 | 09 40.0 |
| 1932 | 6 | 12 33.4 | | 1970 | 5 | 40 43.3 | | 2008 | 5 | 08 44.0 |
| 1933 | 6 | 11 43.2 | | 1971 | 5 | 39 53.0 | | 2009 | 5 | 07 49.0 |
| 1934 | 6 | 10 52.9 | | 1972 | 5 | 39 02.7 | | 2010 | 5 | 06 56.0 |
| 1935 | 6 | 10 02.6 | | 1973 | 5 | 38 12.4 | | 2011 | 5 | 06 04.0 |
| 1936 | 6 | 09 12.4 | | 1974 | 5 | 37 22.2 | | 2012 | 5 | 05 15.0 |
| 1937 | 6 | 08 22.1 | | 1975 | 5 | 36 31.9 | | 2013 | 5 | 04 27.0 |
| 1938 | 6 | 07 31.8 | | 1976 | 5 | 35 41.6 | | 2014 | 5 | 03 41.0 |
| 1939 | 6 | 06 41.6 | | 1977 | 5 | 34 51.3 | | 2015 | 5 | 02 56.0 |

## Table IV

First Correction (Precession and Solar Mutation) to obtain the
True Sidereal Longitude of the S.V.P., calculations being based on the M.S.
All values are subtractive. Compiled by Garth Allen.

| MS | P S | MS | P S | MS | P S | MS | P S |
|---|---|---|---|---|---|---|---|
| 18h 40m | -0.44 | 0h 40m | -12.20 | 6h 40m | -25.55 | 12h 40m | -37.20 |
| 50 | -0.90 | 50 | -12.45 | 50 | -25.99 | 50 | -37.45 |
| 19 00 | -1.36 | 1 00 | -12.70 | 7 00 | -26.43 | 13 00 | -37.69 |
| 10 | -1.81 | 10 | -12.96 | 10 | -26.86 | 10 | -37.95 |
| 20 | -2.25 | 20 | -13.23 | 20 | -27.29 | 20 | -38.20 |
| 30 | -2.69 | 30 | -13.50 | 30 | -27.71 | 30 | -38.47 |
| 40 | -3.12 | 40 | -13.78 | 40 | -28.12 | 40 | -38.74 |
| 50 | -3.54 | 50 | -14.07 | 50 | -28.53 | 50 | -39.02 |
| 20 00 | -3.96 | 2 00 | -14.36 | 8 00 | -28.93 | 14 00 | -39.30 |
| 10 | -4.36 | 10 | -14.67 | 10 | -29.32 | 10 | -39.59 |
| 20 | -4.76 | 20 | -14.97 | 20 | -29.71 | 20 | -39.90 |
| 30 | -5.14 | 30 | -15.30 | 30 | -30.09 | 30 | -40.21 |
| 40 | -5.52 | 40 | -15.63 | 40 | -30.46 | 40 | -40.53 |
| 50 | -5.88 | 50 | -15.97 | 50 | -31.82 | 50 | -40.86 |
| 21 00 | -6.24 | 3 00 | -16.32 | 9 00 | -31.17 | 15 00 | -41.20 |
| 10 | -6.58 | 10 | -16.67 | 10 | -31.52 | 10 | -41.55 |
| 20 | -6.92 | 20 | -17.04 | 20 | -32.85 | 20 | -41.91 |
| 30 | -7.24 | 30 | -17.41 | 30 | -32.18 | 30 | -42.28 |
| 40 | -7.56 | 40 | -17.79 | 40 | -32.50 | 40 | -42.67 |
| 50 | -7.86 | 50 | -18.18 | 50 | -33.81 | 50 | -43.06 |
| 22 00 | -8.16 | 4 00 | -18.58 | 10 00 | -33.11 | 16 00 | -43.46 |
| 10 | -8.44 | 10 | -18.99 | 10 | -33.40 | 10 | -43.87 |
| 20 | -8.72 | 20 | -19.40 | 20 | -33.69 | 20 | -44.29 |
| 30 | -8.99 | 30 | -19.82 | 30 | -33.97 | 30 | -44.72 |
| 40 | -9.26 | 40 | -20.24 | 40 | -34.24 | 40 | -45.15 |
| 50 | -9.52 | 50 | -20.67 | 50 | -34.50 | 50 | -45.59 |
| 23 00 | -9.77 | 5 00 | -21.10 | 11 00 | -35.76 | 17 00 | -46.04 |
| 10 | -10.02 | 10 | -21.54 | 10 | -35.02 | 10 | -46.50 |
| 20 | -10.27 | 20 | -21.98 | 20 | -35.27 | 20 | -46.96 |
| 30 | -10.51 | 30 | -22.43 | 30 | -35.51 | 30 | -47.42 |
| 40 | -10.75 | 40 | -22.88 | 40 | -35.76 | 40 | -47.89 |
| 50 | -10.99 | 50 | -23.32 | 50 | -36.00 | 50 | -48.35 |
| 0 00 | -11.23 | 6 00 | -23.77 | 12 00 | -36.24 | 18 00 | -48.82 |
| 10 | -11.47 | 10 | -24.22 | 10 | -36.48 | 10 | -49.29 |
| 20 | 11.71 | 20 | -24.66 | 20 | -36.72 | 20 | -49.76 |
| 30 | -11.95 | 30 | -25.11 | 30 | -36.96 | 30 | -50.23 |
|  |  |  |  |  |  | 40 | -50.69 |

## Table V

Second Correction to Obtain the True Sidereal Longitude of the S.V.P. Amount of correction is due to the effects of Lunar Nutation, the argument being the mean tropical longitude of the Moon's ascending node.

| Long | N | Long | Long | N | Long | Long | N | Long | Long | N | Long |
|---|---|---|---|---|---|---|---|---|---|---|---|
| 0° | + 0.00 | - 360° | 33 | + 9.20 | - 327 | 66 | + 15.59 | - 294 | 99 | + 17.08 | - 261 |
| 1 | + 0.29 | - 359 | 34 | + 9.45 | - 326 | 67 | + 15.71 | - 293 | 100 | + 17.04 | - 260 |
| 2 | + 0.58 | - 358 | 35 | + 9.69 | - 325 | 68 | + 15.83 | - 292 | 101 | + 16.99 | - 259 |
| 3 | + 0.88 | - 357 | 36 | + 9.94 | - 324 | 69 | + 15.95 | - 291 | 102 | + 16.93 | - 258 |
| 4 | + 1.17 | - 356 | 37 | + 10.17 | - 323 | 70 | + 16.06 | - 290 | 103 | + 16.88 | - 257 |
| 5 | + 1.46 | - 355 | 38 | + 10.41 | - 322 | 71 | + 16.17 | - 289 | 104 | + 16.82 | - 256 |
| 6 | + 1.75 | - 354 | 39 | + 10.64 | - 321 | 72 | + 16.26 | - 288 | 105 | + 16.65 | - 255 |
| 7 | + 2.04 | - 353 | 40 | + 10.87 | - 320 | 73 | + 16.36 | - 287 | 106 | + 16.68 | - 254 |
| 8 | + 2.34 | - 352 | 41 | + 11.10 | - 319 | 74 | + 16.45 | - 286 | 107 | + 16.59 | - 253 |
| 9 | + 2.63 | - 351 | 42 | + 11.32 | - 318 | 75 | + 16.54 | - 285 | 108 | + 16.51 | - 252 |
| 10 | + 2.92 | - 350 | 43 | + 11.55 | - 317 | 76 | + 16.62 | - 284 | 109 | + 16.42 | - 251 |
| 11 | + 3.21 | - 349 | 44 | + 11.77 | - 316 | 77 | + 16.69 | - 283 | 110 | + 16.33 | - 250 |
| 12 | + 3.50 | - 348 | 45 | + 11.98 | - 315 | 78 | + 16.77 | - 282 | 111 | + 16.23 | - 249 |
| 13 | + 3.78 | - 347 | 46 | + 12.19 | - 314 | 79 | + 16.84 | - 281 | 112 | + 16.12 | - 248 |
| 14 | + 4.07 | - 346 | 47 | + 12.40 | - 313 | 80 | + 16.90 | - 280 | 113 | + 16.01 | - 247 |
| 15 | + 4.36 | - 345 | 48 | + 12.60 | - 312 | 81 | + 16.96 | - 279 | 114 | + 15.90 | - 246 |
| 16 | + 4.64 | - 344 | 49 | + 12.81 | - 311 | 82 | + 17.00 | - 278 | 115 | + 15.78 | - 245 |
| 17 | + 4.92 | - 343 | 50 | + 13.00 | - 310 | 83 | + 17.05 | - 277 | 116 | + 15.66 | - 244 |
| 18 | + 5.20 | - 342 | 51 | + 13.19 | - 309 | 84 | + 17.09 | - 276 | 117 | + 15.52 | - 243 |
| 19 | + 5.48 | - 341 | 52 | + 13.38 | - 308 | 85 | + 17.13 | - 275 | 118 | + 15.39 | - 242 |
| 20 | + 5.76 | - 340 | 53 | + 13.56 | - 307 | 86 | + 17.16 | - 274 | 119 | + 15.25 | - 241 |
| 21 | + 6.03 | - 339 | 54 | + 13.75 | - 306 | 87 | + 17.18 | - 273 | 120 | + 15.11 | - 240 |
| 22 | + 6.30 | - 338 | 55 | + 13.92 | - 305 | 88 | + 17.20 | - 272 | 121 | + 14.96 | - 249 |
| 23 | + 6.58 | - 337 | 56 | + 14.09 | - 304 | 89 | + 17.22 | - 271 | 122 | + 14.80 | - 248 |
| 24 | + 6.85 | - 336 | 57 | + 14.26 | - 303 | 90 | + 17.23 | - 270 | 123 | + 14.64 | - 247 |
| 25 | + 7.12 | - 335 | 58 | + 14.42 | - 302 | 91 | + 17.23 | - 269 | 124 | + 14.48 | - 246 |
| 26 | + 7.39 | - 334 | 59 | + 14.59 | - 301 | 92 | + 17.23 | - 268 | 125 | + 14.31 | - 245 |
| 27 | + 7.66 | - 333 | 60 | + 14.74 | - 300 | 93 | + 17.22 | - 267 | 126 | + 14.14 | - 234 |
| 28 | + 7.92 | - 332 | 61 | + 14.89 | - 299 | 94 | + 17.22 | - 266 | 127 | + 13.96 | - 233 |
| 29 | + 8.19 | - 331 | 62 | + 15.04 | - 298 | 95 | + 17.20 | - 265 | 128 | + 13.78 | - 232 |
| 30 | + 8.44 | - 330 | 63 | + 15.18 | - 297 | 96 | + 17.18 | - 264 | 129 | + 13.60 | - 231 |
| 31 | + 8.70 | - 329 | 64 | + 15.33 | - 296 | 97 | + 17.15 | - 263 | 130 | + 13.41 | - 230 |
| 32 | + 8.95 | - 328 | 65 | + 15.46 | - 295 | 98 | + 17.11 | - 262 | 131 | + 13.22 | - 229 |

| *Long* N *Long* | *Long* N *Long* | *Long* N *Long* | *Long* N *Long* |
|---|---|---|---|
| 132 + 13.02 − 228 | 144 + 10.33 − 216 | 156 + 7.16 − 204 | 168 + 3.66 − 192 |
| 133 + 12.81 − 227 | 145 + 10.08 − 215 | 157 + 6.89 − 203 | 169 + 3.35 − 191 |
| 134 + 12.61 − 226 | 146 + 9.83 − 214 | 158 + 6.60 − 202 | 170 + 3.06 − 190 |
| 135 + 12.40 − 225 | 147 + 9.58 − 213 | 159 + 6.31 − 201 | 171 + 2.76 − 189 |
| 136 + 12.19 − 224 | 148 + 9.32 − 212 | 160 + 6.03 − 200 | 172 + 2.45 − 188 |
| 137 + 11.96 − 223 | 149 + 9.07 − 211 | 161 + 5.74 − 199 | 173 + 2.15 − 187 |
| 138 + 11.74 − 222 | 150° + 8.80 − 210° | 162 + 5.46 − 198 | 174 + 1.84 − 186 |
| 139 + 11.51 − 221 | 151 + 8.53 − 209 | 163 + 5.16 − 197 | 175 + 1.54 − 185 |
| 140 + 11.28 − 220 | 152 + 8.27 − 208 | 164 + 4.86 − 196 | 176 + 1.23 − 184 |
| 141 + 11.05 − 219 | 153 + 7.99 − 207 | 165 + 4.57 − 195 | 177 + 0.92 − 183 |
| 142 + 10.81 − 218 | 154 + 7.71 − 206 | 166 + 4.27 − 194 | 178 + 0.62 − 182 |
| 143 + 10.57 − 217 | 155 + 7.44 − 205 | 167 + 3.97 − 193 | 179 + 0.31 − 181 |
| | | | 180 + 0.00 − 180 |

Lightning Source UK Ltd
Milton Keynes UK
UKOW07f0000011217
313661UK00009B/683/P